LIVING ABUNDANTLY AFTER PREGNANCY LOSS

SEEKING Hope

FINDING Joy

HOPE H. DOVER

Published by hope*books
2217 Matthews Township Pkwy
Suite D302
Matthews, NC 28105
www.hopebooks.com

hope*books is a division of hope*media

Printed in the United States of America

First paperback edition.
Paperback ISBN: 979-8-89185-317-1
Hardcover ISBN: 979-8-89185-318-8
Ebook ISBN: 979-8-89185-319-5
Library of Congress Number: 2025944910

Praise for
Seeking Hope, Finding Joy

Believers are called to grieve with hope (1 Thessalonians 4:13), and in this touching and insightful book, Hope Dover helps us navigate the reality of living with pregnancy loss while clinging to the One who provides strength for today and bright hope for tomorrow. Healing balm is available here as she shares her family's story and offers guidance from the perspective of one who knows both the depth of pain and the mercy of a God whose grace is sufficient.

Daniel L. Smoak
Pastor, Westminster Presbyterian Church, Charleston, SC

As Hope's doctor, I witnessed her courage as she navigated her losses. This book illustrates how faith in God, music, and even learning rucking has carried her through this journey. Hope's testament is a moving story of transforming grief into grace. This book will inspire and comfort those walking this path.

Priya Bajaj Pillai, MD

In *Seeking Hope, Finding Joy*, Hope Dover masterfully weaves together personal stories of heartache and loss, biblical encouragement that God can be trusted with our deepest pain, and practical wisdom for navigating life after pregnancy loss. She gives us an example of what it looks like to walk through unimaginable suffering and still grab hold of the abundant life that is available to us in Christ. As a fellow loss mom, these pages made me feel seen, understood, uplifted, and empowered to live abundantly amid trials and grief.

Amanda McMullen
Editor, hope*books
Owner, AsherMarieCo

If you have experienced pregnancy loss or infertility, don't walk through that pain alone. Join Hope Dover on a journey of healing as she tenderly offers companionship through her own story, comfort from the promises of Scripture, and practical ways to remember and heal. Her heartfelt words shine a light of hope on the path toward joy and fullness of life again.

Rebecca Madden
Co-author, *Breathless Haste: Finding God in Ordinary Life*

Hope Dover's *Seeking Hope, Finding Joy: Living Abundantly After Pregnancy Loss* will resonate deeply with every mother who has ever held a negative pregnancy test in her hands. The unique sadness and grief that only an expectant mother experiences are captured beautifully in her words. Hope offers practical guidance for navigating grief as a faith-filled woman, providing gentle encouragement to face the loss rather than avoid it. No matter the circumstances, this book will help women move forward, embrace their grief, and discover hope and joy again.

Carrie Watts
Author, *Crisis of Faith*

As an OB-GYN, I have seen women struggle with a lifelong grief after they experience a pregnancy loss. This grief doesn't go away by having more children but only becomes more complex. In *Seeking Hope, Finding Joy*, Hope Dover gives grieving mothers a sacred space to experience both sorrow and rejoicing after pregnancy loss. This book helps mothers cherish all of their children - both born and unborn. Hope beautifully acknowledges the thread of grief that is permanently woven into a mother's heart after pregnancy loss.

This book gently guides a grieving mother with how to trust God when her pregnancy loss is recent. But this book also cares for the mother who is processing through her loss decades later. Through healing scripture, thoughtful questions, and guided self-reflection, this book will be a treasure for any mother who has experienced pregnancy loss.

Rachelle Keng, MD, FACOG
Author of *Woven in the Womb:*
Peace for the Pregnant and Postpartum Soul
Director of Woven Motherhood, LLC.

For Thomas Roy
The one who made me a mother

For Margaret Rebecca
The one who taught me that it only takes a second to fall in love

For Samuel Harper
The one who showed me joy and sorrow can coexist

For Emma Joy
The one who is proof that God is El Roi

For Keith
The only one who truly understands

Table of Contents

Joy Meets Sorrow

As I sat in the recliner holding my just days-old newborn, the photographer placed a small Gideon camouflage testament in his hands. He hugged the Bible, which didn't seem so small anymore, against his tiny body. I looked down at him and felt tears begin to flood my eyes. I looked up at her and told her I needed a minute. She looked back at me and said she did too.

The small Bible he held was a gift from my Daddy, inscribed with a special message for the baby that so many people helped pray into the world. When I saw my precious miracle holding that Bible, all of the emotions I had felt over the almost three years prior collided with the feelings I had felt since he was born. This moment is seared into my memory. It is one of the first moments I experienced immense joy and immense sorrow at the same time.

In the days and weeks after his birth, I was surprised by how often these opposing feelings showed themselves in the same moment. I didn't know what to do with them. They were at odds with each other. How could I be filled with so much joy and so much heartache at the same time?

There were times I would hold him and just cry. I would cry because I was finally holding my baby, a living child. Over the years, I often wondered if this would ever happen. I had hope, but I also had doubts that having living children would become a reality for me. Holding him brought so much joy.

Other times, I would hold him and cry because I was experiencing the full realization of everything I missed out on with my first two babies. I was reminded of everything I never got to do with them. I never got to hold them. I never got to hear them cry or see them smile. They never fell asleep in my arms as I sang to them. So many moments were stolen by their deaths.

Eleven months passed, and we brought another baby into the world. As I learned the ins and outs of mothering two living children while grieving two babies in heaven, the moments of simultaneous joy and sorrow persisted. I felt like a mess, torn between the grief of then and the joy of now.

Life held so much goodness as I lived out my dream of mothering babies. I loved watching them grow and learn. I took pictures of every little moment, seeing each moment as something to treasure. But I was afraid to be happy because I equated happiness with moving on and forgetting the past.

Life was still difficult at times, too. Grief and sorrow would creep in, sometimes when I least expected. The tears would still stream down my face as I missed my two babies in heaven. And I was afraid to be sad because I equated sadness with not appreciating and recognizing the gifts of the present.

Would it always be like this?

Would joy and sorrow show up together so often?

Would every good moment share memories of my difficult journey to mothering living children?

What was I supposed to do with these mixed emotions?

Why was it so hard?

I struggled with the coexistence of joy and sorrow in the first few years of mothering my living children. I was overwhelmed with grief in moments that I felt should be joyful. There was tension when these moments of joy and sorrow filled the same space. I felt pulled between remembering the past and living in the present.

God met me in this place of tension and guided me in learning how to live fully in it. It took time and a mindset shift for me to reconcile this tension. Now I see the moments of joy and sorrow as a gift. I am grateful for my story and the perspective it gives me. Life is not void of sorrow. I have not forgotten my babies in heaven. My story is still hard. The tension of the conflicting feelings of joy and sorrow is gone because I have found a way to live abundantly in the sacred space where joy and sorrow collide.

Have you felt this tension too? Have you found yourself stuck between the weight of losing your baby and the beauty of the present? Do you wonder how to hold grief and gratitude in the same breath? If you feel this way, I want you to know you are not alone.

This book recounts my journey to learning to live abundantly in joy and sorrow. It invites you to step into that space with me and explore what it means to honor the past while embracing the present. Together, we will seek a path forward. We won't do this by choosing *between* joy and sorrow, but by learning to carry them both.

Are you ready to take that journey with me?

Walking Through These Chapters

S*eeking Hope, Finding Joy: Living Abundantly After Pregnancy Loss* is a blend of memoir, devotional reflection, and spiritual practice born from my experience navigating life after pregnancy loss. Grief is not linear. It is complex, layered, and deeply personal. The structure of this book reflects that truth. Each chapter invites you into the space where personal story, biblical truth, and spiritual reflection meet.

Each chapter contains:

- A core story from my journey of loss, healing, parenting, and faith.
- Reflection and teaching to gently guide you as you process your own story.
- A biblical reflection to frame the experience through the lens of God's presence.
- The closing section (The Abundant Path) has simple, practical steps to hold both sorrow and joy in your everyday life.

Read slowly. Give yourself permission to linger, revisit passages, and rest. This book is not a step-by-step guide for getting over grief. It's a companion in your journey. It won't eliminate the pain or tie your story up in a pretty red bow. It will sit with you in your sorrow and remind you that joy is still possible.

Part One:
The Loss—
Experiencing Brokenness

CHAPTER 1

The Prayer
that Changed Everything

"Trust in the Lord with all your heart, and do not lean on your own understanding. In all your ways acknowledge him, and he will make straight your paths." – Proverbs 3:5-6

I had been in that waiting room too many times to count but never on the side where the pregnant women sat. On this day, I sat alone, but not for long. My husband joined me, and we waited. My obstetrician's office scheduled this appointment with the maternal-fetal medicine specialist after some abnormalities on a recent ultrasound. The maternal-fetal medicine specialists shared an office with the reproductive endocrinologist I had been seeing since my mid-twenties, first for endometriosis, then for infertility. After a long weekend and seemingly longer work day of waiting, we waited again to find out more.

The tech called us back and asked a few questions. She explained that she would do the scan, and the doctor would come in and repeat the scan. She didn't want us to be alarmed when the doctor came in and repeated what she had just done. As the scan began, we heard that beautiful heartbeat we had just heard several days before. She took many measurements and printed out the pictures to show the doctor. Minutes later, a genetic counselor entered the room, introduced herself, and asked several questions before leaving again.

When the genetic counselor returned with the doctor and tech, the doctor quietly repeated the scan. She helped me sit up. Then, she spoke the three words that caused our world to stand still—"It's not good." She went on to explain all the anomalies discovered during the scan. But all I heard was that my baby was not going to live outside my womb. Shock set in, and it felt as if the doctor's words sucked the air out of the room. Tears fell. My husband wailed.

The genetic counselor assured us that nothing I did or was exposed to caused the fatal anomalies. There was no reason. Our baby's body just did not form correctly. Medical professionals presented many unknowns to us on that day. We learned I might or might not make it to term. If I did make it to term, it might or might not be a live birth. One thing they knew for sure. Our baby had **no** chance of life outside of the womb. We had to make an impossible decision that no parent should ever have to make.

As they left the room, they told us to take as long as we needed. After trying to compose ourselves, I called my sister, asking her to find someone and drive to the hospital to get Keith's truck home. I couldn't drive. We eventually made our way to the parking garage and sat in the car waiting for her. The stench of motor oil from the cars and coffee from the coffee shop inside filled the air. The work day was ending, and people hurriedly made their way to their vehicles, going about their lives like any other Monday. We sat silently, watching the world go on as ours had just come to a dead stop.

When my sister and niece arrived, we explained what was going on as best we could between sobs and tears. Words were difficult as we recounted what the doctor had told us about our baby's precious, imperfectly formed body. After a few minutes, we got in our vehicles and pulled out of the parking garage. We had to tell our families. The first stop was my parents' house.

A Father's Prayer

We pulled into my parents' driveway and entered the house. I don't remember the exact words I spoke to tell them their baby girl's child, their precious grandchild, would not live. But I do remember my Mama's cry. As we tried to explain everything we had learned from the specialist about our baby's broken body, my sister arrived. She was followed by my niece and brother-in-law.

We filled their small sunroom, the core of our family, minus my middle sister, who lives out of state, trying to make sense of the unthinkable. We cried many tears and asked questions that didn't have answers. How did this happen? Why did this happen? What are we going to do? How are we going to make this decision? Is it wrong if we choose to end our baby's life?

We didn't answer those questions that day. Some of them still linger. In this uncertainty, one thing became clear—Who we would turn to to get us through this horrific nightmare.

Before we left, my Daddy prayed—and everything changed. I sat in the recliner with Keith across from me. My family gathered around, laid their hands upon us, and covered us in prayer. I don't remember the exact words of Daddy's prayer that day. The words themselves did not matter.

Daddy couldn't tell us why this was happening. No one could. He didn't understand any more than we did. We were all in shock. One thing Daddy did know was that none of us could make it through this on our own. The prayer he prayed that day reflected his unwavering faith, just as all the prayers I had heard him pray my entire life had done. He knew that we would need the resurrection power of Jesus to get us through.

While much of that day is a blur, this moment is clear in my memory. As I sat surrounded by the people who love me the most, I felt the Holy Spirit fall upon me. At that moment, as words from a hurting father were sent to the Father, I knew it would be okay. I was still devastated, my heart ripped in two, but I knew we would make it through. I was beginning to feel a peace beyond all understanding.

In the few years before this day, I had not been walking the Christian walk expected of us as followers of Christ. My relationship with Jesus was lacking. We weren't in church regularly. I rarely cracked open my Bible, and I only prayed when I needed something.

When the doctor said, "It's not good," I had nowhere else to go but my knees, nowhere else to turn but my faith. Now, that faith, which was so weak, was being put through the ultimate test. My Daddy's prayer was like a compass, pointing us in the direction we needed to go to face the impossible path before us. He pointed us to Jesus, as he has done my entire life.

When Life Feels Out of Control

After we left my parents' house, my other sister called me again, pointing me to Jesus. We made our way to tell Keith's parents. The details are a blur. When we got home from telling them, I called a few more friends, then suffered through a sleepless night. The next day, I could not bear hearing myself repeat the words, so I sent texts and emails explaining the situation and asking for prayer.

A grief like no other took hold of me when I learned my baby was going to die. My world stopped turning, and I had no idea how it would ever start spinning again. I felt sick to my stomach at times. Other times, I felt numb. In the days, weeks, and months that followed, I would wake up and have to remind myself that this was not a dream. I was really living this nightmare.

We were thrown into a situation we never imagined we'd face. It is one of those situations where you cannot say what you would do until you are in the middle. We believed (and still believe) in the sanctity of life. Terminating a pregnancy was never a decision that would need a second thought. That was not an option. I had not planned to have any prenatal genetic screenings. It did not matter how our baby came out or if our baby wasn't going to be "normal"—we were going to love the baby no matter what. Then we were hit with those words: "universally not compatible with life." And suddenly, everything was different.

I knew where I stood on the topic of abortion. I believed life was sacred and that it was not our place as humans to decide when it ends. Suddenly, those beliefs were colliding with reality. Nothing was as clear as it once seemed.

In the days that followed, I had multiple conversations with the genetic counselor and with trusted doctors. Even though they all assured me nothing I did caused these abnormalities, I replayed every moment of the pregnancy in my mind, wondering if there was anything I could have done differently. I searched the internet for answers and found none. The moments that weren't filled with sobbing left me numb inside, yet the prayers, calls, visits, and cards comforted me.

Days later, we had made our decision for the most part, but we wanted one more ultrasound just to confirm what the specialist had told us. We found ourselves in another waiting room, sitting in silence. We were not expecting a miracle or a different prognosis. We wanted to have all the information available before making our final decision.

Leading up to the appointment, I prayed for God to take the decision away. I prayed for God to take my baby's life so I wouldn't have to decide that a doctor would do it. As the scan began, and we heard the sound of our baby's heartbeat that was so sweet just a month before, I knew God had not answered my prayer. Keith squeezed my hand as tears fell down our faces. I asked the technician to turn off the sound, closed my eyes, and waited for it to be over.

My doctor confirmed what the specialist and genetic counselor had told us. Our baby, whom we later named Thomas Roy, would not live outside my womb. She expressed her concern over my trying to carry the baby to term. My health was at risk. She did not pressure us towards one decision. She shared the hard facts of what was happening and did it compassionately.

Why was He putting this decision in our hands, conflicting with all we believed?

Why could He not just take the choice away?

Why did our baby's heart still have to be beating?

Hearing my baby's heartbeat and coming to terms with the fact that God was not going to take this burden away was the moment I began to realize I was not the author of my story. I was not in control. Over the months and years that followed, I learned even more about how little control I had. We struggled to get pregnant again. When we did, I experienced a miscarriage, followed by more fertility issues. Indeed, I was not in control.

I was left wondering if I would ever get to be a mother to living children. The way my heart was ripped in two every month I stared at a negative pregnancy test left me worn and weary. I knew God had given me the desire to be a mother, and I didn't understand why it was so hard. Month after month, I prayed for a baby, and month after month, I was left with empty arms.

I reached the point where there was nothing left to do but surrender.

The Long Road of Surrender

Surrendering to God and trusting His plan didn't come quickly. It didn't happen overnight. In the years leading up to the loss, I attempted to control things that were entirely out of my control. I thought that if I planned well enough, I could handle whatever came my way. Losing Thomas Roy on May 18, 2012, shattered that perspective. While the loss brought the head knowledge that nothing was in my control, it still took several years to surrender all control to God. I still held on to the fear of letting go.

At times, surrendering everything to God felt freeing. The pressure to have it all figured out and under control was gone. I didn't have to worry about tomorrow because tomorrow was already in God's hands.

Other times, handing my dream of mothering living children over to God felt like giving up on the dream. What if mothering living children wasn't in God's plans? What if all He had for me was a lifetime of grief?

I had to make a daily decision to surrender everything to God. In the months following Thomas Roy's death, I had to wake up every day and remind myself that it was not a dream. He was gone. All we had experienced had actually happened. This new reality was my life. Waking up to this new reality every day served as a reminder that I was not in control.

Pregnancy announcements were excruciating. I had to turn my head at the sight of a pregnant woman or newborn baby. I wasn't unhappy for these women, nor did I hate the sight of babies. Seeing these things left me doubting God's plan. I didn't understand why this was the road before me.

I clung to Jeremiah 29:11, "'For I know the plans I have for you,' declares the Lord, 'plans to prosper you and not to harm you, plans to give you hope and a future'" (NIV). In times of doubt, I repeated this verse, reminding myself that God had a plan, even when I could not understand what was happening. Many times, my belief in this Old Testament promise was the only thing that got me through another day.

Surrendering to God was something I had to return to over and over. It was a daily choice. Some days, resting in God's plan was easy. Other days, I had to fight for it. I also had to fight not to try to control things. Watching other people live the life I so desperately wanted was hard. Every month that brought a negative pregnancy test also brought the temptation to take control.

We tried infertility treatments to no avail. Then we finally saw two pink lines on a pregnancy test again one June morning. We were elated to be in this place again, experiencing the hope of a new baby. I went in for a blood test on a Monday to confirm the pregnancy. On Friday of the same week, I was back in the reproductive endocrinologist's office for more blood tests to confirm a miscarriage.

Suddenly, we were back to where we started, only that time we had two dead babies, even more rips in our hearts, and still empty arms.

Everything was out of my control, and I had no choice but to surrender it to God.

After we lost our second baby, Margaret Rebecca, we continued to try for a pregnancy. I began to share more about our struggles outside of my circle of family and close friends. In addition to my prayers, I asked others to pray before infertility procedures. During the months we didn't do infertility treatments, I prayed for God to show his power and give us a baby. Still, month after month, I stared at one pink line.

Surrender meant trusting God, even when my prayers were seemingly going unanswered. I was slowly learning that trust is built in the letting go.

A Biblical Example of Surrender: Hannah's Story

In 1 Samuel 1, we meet Elkanah, who has two wives. His wife Hannah had no children, but his wife Peninnah did. Hannah was a sorrowful, desperate, and misunderstood woman.

In biblical times, the ability to bear children was a sign of success for women. Children were seen as assets vital to the survival of the family. Barrenness was sometimes seen as the result of sin and brought shame to the infertile woman and her family.[1] Hannah's barrenness may be the reason Elkanah took a second wife.[2]

Hannah desperately wanted to have a child. 1 Samuel 1 tells us that Peninnah ridiculed Hannah due to her barrenness, which caused Hannah to weep and not eat. Elkanah could not understand Hannah's sorrow, asking why she was so sad.

Imagine how Hannah must have felt in her inability to conceive a child. To top it all off, she gets ridiculed by her husband's other wife, who has everything she's ever wanted. The pain of watching someone live out her dream must have been excruciating. The emotional and social toll her barrenness took had to have been overwhelming.

What did Hannah do when her sorrow threatened to get the best of her? Instead of letting her grief harden her heart, Hannah prayed and brought her pain to the only One who could carry it. And that prayer changed everything for her.

In her desperation, she went to the temple and poured her heart out to God. She not only asked God for what she desired. Hannah surrendered everything to God, vowing to give this child she so desired to the Lord if He opened her womb. She placed her future in God's hands by offering the very thing she longed for.

Something shifted after her prayer of surrender. This shift wasn't in her circumstances, but in her spirit. Verse 18 tells us she left the temple and ate, "and her face was no longer sad." Hannah didn't surrender after her desire for a child had been fulfilled. She surrendered, trusting God would hear and answer her prayer. She gave God everything, including the child she wanted so badly, before she knew her story's direction.

Hannah's circumstances didn't change right away. She was still barren when she left the temple. She walked away from the temple in faith, believing God heard her prayer. The peace Hannah felt after surrender enabled her to trust what she could not see. Surrendering it all to God, trusting Him, and walking in faith changed her heart.

God didn't forget Hannah. His plan was unfolding, even though she couldn't see it. God's response to Hannah's surrender was to give her the child she desired: "And Elkanah knew Hannah his wife, and the LORD remembered her. And in due time Hannah conceived and bore a son, and she called his name Samuel, for she said, 'I have asked for him from the LORD'" (1 Samuel 1:19-20). Hannah's surrender and trust positioned her to receive God's faithfulness in His timing. This faithfulness isn't always immediate, but it is always certain.

It is important to note that Hannah's peace came after she surrendered to God, not after her desires were fulfilled. Her peace didn't come because she got what she wanted. Her peace came because she learned to trust God fully.

The idea of experiencing peace by surrendering everything and trusting God completely can feel counterintuitive, especially when we like to be in control. Prayer, surrender, and trust can bring peace, even before our prayers are answered. Giving everything to God brings us closer to Him.

Have you ever experienced peace before your prayers were answered? What is something you are clinging tightly to? What would it look like to release that to God, like Hannah did?

What Surrender Looks Like in Everyday Life

Like Hannah, I had to learn to live a life of surrender, which didn't come easily. Surrendering control to God did not mean grief went away, and the pain of losing my babies disappeared. Surrender meant I stopped trying to control what my healing looked like and how my story would unfold.

There were moments in my grief that I had to actively choose to surrender. Every month that passed after Thomas Roy's death was a reminder that he was gone and I was not in control. Each time I saw only one line on a pregnancy test, I was forced to place my dream of mothering living children in God's hands.

I learned there is no right or wrong way to grieve. As part of my surrender, I had to allow myself to feel the pain without pushing it away. I had to be okay with not having all of the answers. I also had to change how I viewed my future. My prayers to God changed from "God, give us a child" to "God, if it is Your will, give us a child." This shift allowed me to let go of my expectations and be open to God's plan.

This shift was hard because I expected surrender to bring immediate relief from the pain, but it didn't. The pain and the fear were still there. Life after loss was hard for a very long time. At times, it is still hard. Surrendering didn't remove the hard things but allowed me to be held in them.

Surrender helped me endure instead of merely survive. Enduring looked like trusting God with the next step when I couldn't see the road ahead.

Trust often happens in the quiet, ordinary moments. It's not always big and bold. Sometimes it's whispering a prayer when fear sneaks in or not comparing your story to someone else's. Trust shows up in small, daily rhythms like reading scripture and recording your worries in a journal.

There are moments when trust is challenged. For me, these challenges came on due date anniversaries or special days like Mother's Day. Seeing a pregnant woman in the grocery store or reading a post on social media where a mother was complaining about her children caused me to question God's plan. I had to learn to pause and give myself grace in these moments.

When my living children were born, I had to learn to trust and surrender in a different way. When I was pregnant with my son, I worried I was going to be an anxious, overprotective mama. Just as I had to surrender control of my dreams of motherhood, I had to relinquish control in parenting after loss. I had to trust God with the baby now in my arms.

I still have moments where I am tempted to question God's plan. Grief shows up on ordinary days and causes me to wonder how things could have been different. I question why my story had to unfold the way it did. I long for all four of my children to be here with me.

It shows up in ordinary moments as I cook dinner, watch my children play, or fold laundry. In these moments, I must choose presence over fear and gratitude over resentment. I have to choose to be content with what I have instead of what I long to have. As my story unfolds, I remind myself that I can't see the whole picture of God's plan.

This became a daily act of surrender that helped me parent with confidence, knowing God is in control. Trusting God allowed more joy into motherhood. It enabled me to release my expectations of what should be and enjoy being a mama.

There is no formula for surrender. You don't have to have it all figured out. The path to surrender is made up of quiet, faithful steps. Are you willing to take one small step toward trust today?

The Abundant Path: Surrendering Control and Trusting God

The path to living abundantly after loss is deeply personal. Everyone will walk it differently, and that's okay. Each chapter ends with a section called The Abundant Path. Don't think of these suggestions as tasks to check off. I want you to see them as invitations to engage, reflect, and take small steps towards abundant living.

Surrendering control and choosing to trust God doesn't come easily, or all at once. These steps are here to guide your journey. Wherever you are today, I pray they help draw you closer to the One who is always walking beside you.

Name What You're Still Carrying

Pause and identify something you are still holding tightly. What do you feel pressure to manage or protect? Maybe you fear losing another child. You may be experiencing guilt over not being able to protect the baby you lost. Do you have anxiety over parenting your living children "right" because you know what it's like to live without one (or more) of your children?

Naming this burden is a brave act of mothering. Name it with open hands, not clenched fists.

Write a Prayer of Surrender

Write a prayer of surrender from your unique place as a mother whose heart holds both joy and sorrow. You don't need to feel ready to surrender to write this prayer. You only need to be willing to begin.

Here are a few prompts if you need help getting started:

- "God, I don't know how to hold all of this ..."
- "I'm scared to trust You with this part of my story ..."
- "Help me love without fear ..."
- "Help me release what I cannot control ..."

Practice a Posture of Open Hands

Sit in prayer with open hands as a symbol of surrender. This posture helps reinforce what the heart is practicing. It reminds you visually and physically that you are not in control.

As you sit and pray, release specific things to God. What are you most afraid to let go of right now? Picture yourself placing these fears and pressures into God's hands. Can you imagine God receiving it gently, with compassion and free of judgment?

This practice can help replace fear with physical peace, especially if you are always in alert mode.

Anchor to Truth When Trust Feels Weak

Choose a scripture that speaks to God's care for your children, both here and in heaven. Write it down and keep it close by. Read it when anxiety is high and trust feels weak to help anchor yourself in truth.

Here are some suggested verses:

- Psalm 139:13-16 shows God's intimate knowledge of every child.
- Isaiah 41:10 reminds us that God is always with us.

- Jeremiah 29:11 assures us of God's hopeful plans for our future.

Create a Visual of Trust and Remembrance

As a mother who holds both joy and sorrow, keeping a visual of trust and remembrance in your space can be healing. This can be something that reminds you of both the child(ren) you have lost and your ongoing surrender to God's story for your life. This can help acknowledge your motherhood in all its fullness. It can help you remember and release at the same time.

Here are some suggestions:

- Create or purchase a stone, charm, or bracelet that represents peace, trust, or your child's memory. This is something you can hold during anxious moments.

- Print or write out a phrase to help you re-center when you feel control slipping away. Some examples include: "You're still writing my story." "I trust You with what I can't see." "You are faithful, even here."

This step doesn't need to be elaborate or public. This visual can remind you that you are a mother to all of your children and God is holding each of them, and you, with love.

Think Back to a Moment You Tried to Hold it All Together

Think back to a moment you tried to manage, fix, or control something that felt too uncertain or painful. This moment could have occurred in your grief, during infertility, in parenting after loss, or in everyday moments of anxiety. This is about noticing how deeply we long for certainty, especially after loss. It is not about regret.

- Ask yourself: Was there a moment I tried to make things feel "safe" again after loss? Maybe through planning, protecting, or striving?

- Did I ever put pressure on myself to control the timing of another pregnancy, how I grieved, or how others responded to my grief?

- What did this experience teach me about control and the invitation to trust bGod instead?

Know you are not alone in this. Control can feel like the only way to keep your heart from breaking again. Healing can begin when we recognize that strength is not found in managing outcomes. It is found in trusting God even when we do not understand.

Invite Someone to Walk With You

Surrender is deeply personal, but you don't have to do it alone. Reach out to a trusted friend, fellow loss mom, or mentor. This should be someone who will hold space for your entire motherhood story—your children in heaven and the ones in your arms. Inviting someone to walk with you can help you feel supported as you learn to let go.

Ideas for starting the conversation:

- "I'm having a hard day. Can you pray for me?"

- "There's part of my motherhood story I've never talked about, but I want to start sharing."

- "I'm learning to trust God in new ways. Can I tell you about it?"

I know it can be scary to reach out, especially if you have been met with silence in the past. You deserve to be supported in your surrender, not just in your strength.

Choosing to look to Jesus in troubled times and surrender it all to Him doesn't happen all at once. Sometimes it's not even a conscious choice. It's receiving a prayer prayed over you. It's accepting the offer of wise counsel. Sometimes, it's meekly offering up your own prayer, and other times it's being carried by the many prayers of others. There are times when there are no words, just sobs and tears.

Surrender is possible, even if you don't feel ready. God is near, even if all you have to offer are sobs and tears. This is a place where surrender can begin. God sees you. He holds you. And He is walking with you on the path to abundant life that begins with surrender.

CHAPTER 2

Faith in the Storm

*"When you pass through the waters, I will be with you; and
through the rivers, they shall not overwhelm you; when you walk
through fire you shall not be burned, and the flame shall not
consume you." – Isaiah 43:2*

When we received the devastating diagnosis—that our
baby would not live outside my womb—we were not
attending church regularly. We did not have a church
that we called home anymore. We didn't have a pastor.

My sister asked if we would like her pastor to come and talk
with us. We had never met him before, but the afternoon after the
diagnosis, he showed up at our house armed with pages of scripture he had printed out and a heart to offer us hope. One of the
pages held a printout of the painting *Christ in the Storm on the Sea
of Galilee* by Rembrandt Van Rijn, along with the words of Mark
4:35-41:

On that day, when evening had come, he said to them, "Let us go across to the other side." And leaving the crowd, they took him with them in the boat, just as he was. And other boats were with him. And a great windstorm arose, and the waves were breaking into the boat, so that the boat was already filling. But he was in the stern, asleep on the cushion. And they woke him and said to him, "Teacher, do you not care that we are perishing?" And he awoke and rebuked the wind and said to the sea, "Peace! Be still!" And the wind ceased, and there was a great calm. He said to them, "Why are you so afraid? Have you still no faith?" And they were filled with great fear and said to one another, "Who then is this, that even the wind and the sea obey him?"

I was familiar with the story of Jesus calming the storm. I had heard it since I was a child. Jesus and the disciples were on a boat in the Sea of Galilee. Jesus was sleeping. A violent storm appeared, sending the disciples into a frenzy. The disciples woke Jesus up, and He calmed the storm. Then He scolded the disciples for their diminished faith.

Sitting in our living room that Tuesday afternoon, this pastor, whom we had just met, explained how Rembrandt's painting is a good interpretation of this passage of scripture.

Scan the QR code to view *Christ in the Storm on the Sea of Galilee.*

When the painting is divided in half, there is darkness and light. This shows that hard times will come. This is represented by the darkness. We have hope in the hard times, as represented by the light.

Jesus is sleeping in the middle of the darkness. He is closest to the one struggling the most, which shows that Jesus is with us in the darkness.

The boat is headed toward the light. In the scripture, Jesus says, "Peace! Be still!" The wind stops, and the storm ceases. This represents hope and the power Jesus has in the storm.

Fourteen people are on the boat: Jesus, the twelve disciples, and the artist. Rembrandt painted himself in the picture to show us that this miracle isn't just something that happened thousands of years ago. His appearance in the boat symbolizes us in the boat with Jesus during life's storms.[3]

Again, we were being pointed to Jesus in our storm, to hope and the Light. I held onto those printed-out pages of hope the pastor brought that day and referred to them often in the days and weeks following the diagnosis. They reminded me of my hope in Jesus through the worst storm of my life.

Over the following months, the pastor we met in our darkest hour became our pastor. He and his wife played an integral role in my healing. They ministered to us a year later when we lost our second baby and throughout our struggles to get pregnant again.

They rejoiced with us at the news of another pregnancy. He came to the hospital the day after my son was born and baptized him when he was two and a half months old. They were not only companions in our grief and present in our healing journey, but they also shared in our redemption story.

The Raging Storm— Wrestling with Faith in Chaos

The days following the diagnosis held a multitude of feelings. I was overwhelmed with sadness. I cried until I didn't think there were any more tears to cry, and then I cried some more. I had moments of shock and disbelief that this was our reality. I mostly felt confused. I didn't understand any of it.

Why us?

Why did our baby have to die?

Why did this have to happen during my first pregnancy?

Why were we being left with this impossible decision?

The feelings of sadness, shock, and confusion overwhelmed me. I cycled through these emotions every day until I eventually felt numb. Then, I would get up and do it all over again the next day. Sadness. Shock. Confusion. Numbness. Rinse and repeat.

Faith felt more like a soft whisper, not a strong anchor during this time. Faith felt thin when the numbness set in each day after cycling through sadness, shock, and confusion. I was reaching, but I was unsure I had anything to hold onto. There were times when God felt silent.

Was He there?

Was He hearing my prayers?

Was He listening to the prayers of others on my behalf?

Deep down, I believed the answer to these questions was yes, even though it didn't always feel like it.

In Chapter 1, I wrote about surrendering control and how I slowly came to terms with the truth that I am not the author of my story. But here, in the days following the diagnosis, surrender wasn't just about letting go of control. It was about trying to survive when all I could see was a storm that refused to calm.

As humans, we tend to want to fix things. We want to understand the situation, take control, and handle it ourselves. We spend our days solving problems and are knocked off our feet when something happens that we cannot control.

That's exactly how it felt. I prayed for God to take the decision away. If we didn't have the burden of choosing whether or not to end the pregnancy, maybe it would make our situation a little more bearable. Losing our baby would still be devastating, but not having to make this heartbreaking, impossible decision ourselves might have felt a little easier to carry.

I wanted more than anything for God to calm the storm by taking the decision from us. But He didn't calm the storm. The decision still loomed, and the waves still crashed. Losing control began to feel a lot like losing hope. The more I realized how little control I had over the situation, the less hopeful I felt. My hope was slipping away. Though small, my hope remained. It was strengthened with every call, text, and card that held the prayers of God's people.

I learned that control and surrender are often at odds with each other. In that battle, faith can feel fragile. What if surrender in the storm is not weakness, but the beginning of anchored faith? What if choosing to trust God when the storm won't stop is what anchors us?

The Sea of Galilee painting reminds me of this tension. The storm is raging while Jesus is sleeping, and the disciples are panicking. But Jesus is still there. His presence doesn't make the storm disappear, but it can anchor our souls.

The Role of Anchored Faith

I was facing the biggest storm of my life. I had never felt sorrow like this before. Faith came easily when life was good. Up until this point, life was not perfect, but it had never held this level of pain and lack of control. I had bought into the lie that life would be free of suffering if I were a follower of Jesus.

Over the weeks and months following the diagnosis and death of Thomas Roy, I remained stuck in the cycle of sadness, shock, confusion, and numbness. Everything blurred together. Life felt empty and disconnected as I went through the motions of day-to-day tasks. As I cried myself to sleep one night, I realized that my faith had to go deeper than my emotions. I was not exempt from suffering. The pain wasn't going away. Neither was my lack of control over the situation. I would have to look outside of myself to get through this. I needed a faith rooted in something more substantial than my feelings.

I realized there are two types of faith. I call them emotional faith and anchored faith. Emotional faith is reactive and based on feelings. When life is good, faith is strong. This type of faith isn't a bad thing. It's just not sufficient when life falls apart. And everyone, at some point, will experience life falling apart. Anchored faith is steady and rooted in the unchanging nature of God. Faith is strong because we have an understanding of who God is. Anchored faith doesn't change based on how we are feeling. When the storms of life come and our faith is anchored, we know who to turn to for help.

Surrendering to God meant I had to find an anchored faith rather than the emotional faith I had relied on for most of my life. A few months after Thomas Roy's death, we began attending church again. I started reading my Bible regularly. I memorized scripture. My prayer life became stronger. As I grew closer to God, my faith became more and more anchored.

I began to rely on what the Scriptures say about who God is. As I studied the Bible, I was reminded of these things:

- God is unchangeable (Hebrews 13:8). God is constant and dependable, even when our circumstances are not. We can trust Him.
- God is faithful (Lamentations 3:2-23). When we are in a season of doubt, we can lean into His faithfulness.
- God is sovereign (Isaiah 46:9-10). When life feels out of control, we can rest in knowing God is in control.
- God is good (Psalm 100:5). When we believe in the goodness of God, we can trust that He is working all things for our good and His glory.
- God is love (Romans 5:8). When we know God loves us, we don't feel abandoned, even when He feels silent.

As I rooted my faith in who God is, I slowly became enveloped in a peace beyond my circumstances and understanding. The storm was still raging. I was still grieving my baby's death. I was struggling with infertility and eventually faced the death of another baby. Life wasn't better. I had every reason to crawl under the covers and never get out of bed. Some days, that was exactly what I wanted to do.

I was able to keep moving forward through my grief. I chose to rely on my anchored faith, which was present despite the storm. I sought out hope. My hope became bigger than my circumstances. While I still grieved my losses, I began to develop the belief that God would use my situation for good.

Not Alone in the Storm

In learning to rely on anchored faith, I also had to learn that I was not alone in my pain. Even though there were times when God felt silent, His presence was there, anchoring me even when I couldn't feel it. In Mark 4, we see the disciples panic in the storm. Jesus was in the boat with them, and they still panicked in the chaos. I, too, had moments of panic, even though God was always with me in my personal storm.

Just as I had to stay rooted in the knowledge of who God is, I had to hold fast to the promise that He is always with me. I relied on scriptures like Matthew 28:20, where Jesus says, "I am with you always," and Isaiah 41:10, where God instructs, "Fear not, for I am with you."

Even though God was with me in my grief, there were times I felt alone and misunderstood. Grief can feel lonely and isolating. Pregnancy loss still wasn't widely talked about when Thomas Roy died. Neither was termination for medical reasons. There were times I felt so alone in my grief. Up to that point in my life, I had never experienced such suffering and pain. I had no reference point for the things I was feeling. I sometimes wondered if I was crazy for feeling how I felt.

In November 2012, just days before Thomas Roy's due date and Thanksgiving, I attended a workshop for parents who had gone through pregnancy loss. It was hosted by a local organization called KinderMourn that supports grieving parents and children. The workshop topic was surviving the holidays after loss. There were only a handful of participants in attendance that night. We all had a chance to tell our stories and talk about how we were feeling.

For the first time in six months, I felt seen. In hearing the stories and experiences of others walking through pregnancy loss, I realized I was not crazy. And, most importantly, I realized I was not alone. While the circumstances of each of our losses differed, the aftermath was the same. We were all left with empty arms.

In the following months, I attended support groups facilitated by professional counselors at KinderMourn. I formed relationships with other loss moms as we worked through our grief. Through conversations with other loss moms and the counsel of professionals, I learned the feelings I was feeling were normal. These weekly sessions helped form the foundation of my grief journey.

Being in community with other loss moms helped me move forward in my grief. These weekly sessions spent sitting on the couch in the upstairs room of the KinderMourn home served as a safe haven for me to process all that had happened and how I was feeling. Each conversation, every head nod in agreement and understanding, helped me feel less alone.

We were not meant to go through life's trials in isolation. In fact, isolation is the enemy of healing. We need others to walk the road of grief alongside us. When we walk with others, we feel seen. We are no longer isolated in our grief. Community is the antidote to loneliness.

A Biblical Example of Anchored Faith: Paul's Shipwreck

We can find an example of anchored faith in the book of Acts. Paul has been wrongly accused by Jewish leaders of teaching against Jewish laws and customs (Acts 21:28), bringing Gentiles into the temple, thus defiling it (Acts 21:28-29), and stirring up riots among the Jews (Acts 24:5). None of the Roman officials he appears before can find him guilty of any crime deserving death. Realizing he won't receive justice locally and understanding that God was calling him to Rome, Paul appeals to Caesar (Acts 25:11) and finds himself on a ship headed to Italy.

In Acts 27, we see that they run into dangerous weather as the journey progresses. Paul warns them of the dangers if they continue sailing, but the centurion does not listen to Paul, and they continue. They are met with a violent storm that lasts for weeks. They began to throw things overboard to stay afloat and lose all hope of survival.

In the middle of the storm, Paul displays anchored faith while everyone else panics in fear. Paul stood to lose everything—his mission and life—yet remained calm. In Acts 27:23–24, Paul says, "For this very night there stood before me an angel of the God to whom I belong and whom I worship, and he said, 'Do not be afraid, Paul; you must stand before Caesar. And behold, God has granted you all those who sail with you.'"

Paul is aware of the danger. He is not denying the existence and severity of the storm. Yet he anchors himself in God's promise. He tells his fellow passengers, "So take heart, men, for I have faith in God that it will be exactly as I have been told" (Acts 27:25). He becomes a calm voice amid chaos. His faith is rooted in God's word and not his circumstances. This faith not only benefits him; it benefits those around him as he sets an example of staying rooted in God.

Paul chose to believe God, even when everything around him was falling apart. This response wasn't reactive. It was grounded in what he already knew about God. Anchored faith is cultivated before the storm and also chosen over and over again in the storm.

You may not feel like a Paul right now. You may feel like a panicked sailor, and that's okay. Anchored faith does not have to feel strong to be real. You can choose to hold onto God's word with shaking knees and trembling hands.

The Abundant Path: Walking in Anchored Faith

Choosing anchored faith in the middle of a storm is a courageous step toward healing. Here are some practical ways to walk in anchored faith. Remember, these are invitations to engage, reflect, and take small steps towards abundant living rather than a set of tasks to check off.

Name Your Storm

Naming the storm does not give it power. Naming the storm helps bring it into the light. What feels emotionally, physically, and spiritually overwhelming right now? Is there a situation, fear, or emotion you need to acknowledge before God today? Name these storms and record them in a journal.

Remember Who is in the Boat

Take another look at Rembrandt's painting *Christ in the Storm on the Sea of Galilee* (see page 23 for the QR code). Find Jesus in the boat. Now visualize Jesus in the middle of your storm. Remember that even when Jesus feels silent, He is still with you. Record how it feels to have Jesus in the boat with you.

Anchor Faith in God's Character

When life's storms hit, it's crucial to have an anchored faith that is steady and rooted in who God is, rather than an emotional faith that is reactive and based on feelings.

Use these prayer prompts to pray through the attributes of God in your storm.

God is Unchangeable (Hebrews 13:8)

> *God, Everything feels uncertain in this storm, but You remain the same. While everything feels unsteady, help me anchor myself in the truth that You never change.*

God is Faithful (Lamentations 3:22-23)

> *Lord, Today I wonder if I'll make it through this storm, but I know You have never left me. Help me remember that Your faithfulness has not run out and is new every morning.*

God is Sovereign (Isaiah 46:9-10)

> *God, I don't know why this happened or where this storm will lead me. But I know You do. Help me rest in knowing You are in control when I am not.*

God is Good (Psalm 100:5)

> *Lord, Life doesn't feel good right now. Help me see glimpses of Your goodness in the middle of this storm.*

God is Love (Romans 5:8)

Jesus, Thank You for loving me in the middle of this grief. When I feel unseen or forgotten, help me remember that Your love has not left me.

Speak Scripture Over the Storm

Biblical truth is a great weapon to combat fear, lies, and despair. God's Word can help anchor us when our emotions are unstable. The following scriptures can help anchor your faith, calm your anxiety, and help you remember God's presence.

Isaiah 41:10

Psalm 46:1-2

Matthew 28:20b

Hebrews 6:19

Lamentations 3:22-23

John 16:33

- Choose one verse to memorize each week.
- Keep a copy of the verse on your mirror, in your journal, on your phone's lock screen, or by your bedside table.
- Pray the verse out loud in anxious or quiet moments.

Surrender Control Daily

Surrender doesn't just happen in one big moment. It must become a daily practice. Anchored faith requires intentional surrender, not emotional certainty. Surrendering control in the middle of the storm may look like letting go of needing answers, giving God control of the timeline, or trusting God when you don't feel like it.

Name one thing to surrender to God each day. Write it down in your journal. Then verbally offer it to God by saying, "God, I release this to You today." This is a small, daily act of surrender and trust.

Let Others In

Grief is hard, especially when we grieve alone. Finding a community that helps you feel seen and understood helps usher in healing. Grieving in community will not remove the storm but will provide company in the boat as you weather the storm. Here are some ways to find community in grief:

- Find one trusted friend or family member to confide in and call or text them. You can simply say, "This is hard. Can we talk?"

- Find a local support group. These groups can help reduce isolation and normalize feelings. Contact your OB-GYN to find out if there are organizations near you that provide support groups for women who have experienced pregnancy loss.

- Find a virtual support group. There are many online groups if there are no support groups near you. See the "Moving Forward: Tools for the Journey" section in the back of the book for a list of national organizations that provide online support groups for women who have experienced pregnancy loss.

- Ask a friend to check in weekly. Sometimes reaching out for help feels hard. Ask a friend to check in with you weekly via text or call. This takes the pressure off you to initiate connection.

In the years since I received that printout of Rembrandt's painting and Mark 4, I have often pulled them out and revisited the imagery of Jesus with me in the storm. My eyes fill with tears of gratitude as I reflect on all those who jumped in the boat with me and stayed until the waters calmed.

Choosing anchored faith was not a one-time decision. It is a choice I have had to continue to make over the years. If your faith feels fragile, be reminded that Jesus is with you and hold on to Him. Anchored faith can be small and steady. Start small and choose one way to anchor your faith today.

CHAPTER 3

The Day I Didn't Die

"Be gracious to me, O Lord, for I am in distress;
my eye is wasted from grief;
my soul and my body also."
– Psalm 31:9

"I wish I had died on that operating table!"

I stood in our bedroom and screamed to my husband in a fit of grief, anger, and despair. He sat speechless, not knowing how to help me in that moment of raw honesty. Life was full of sorrow after losing two babies. It was also full of frustration after countless failed infertility treatments. We waited for a pregnancy month after month, and we continued to face the disappointment of seeing only one pink line on the pregnancy tests.

While I wasn't in any danger of harming myself when I spoke those words, they were true. I was hurting. The sorrow was lingering. And the pain was unbearable.

Life felt hopeless.

Details of the worst day of my life resurfaced often.

Grief had taken over my life, and I had grown weary.

The years between the deaths of my babies and the births of my living children were really dark at times. Most of the time, my grief went unacknowledged by others. The cards, calls, and texts had stopped. I was walking around with an invisible wound unnoticeable to most.

On the outside, I tried to make it seem like I had it all together and was handling my grief well. I put a smile on my face in an attempt to hide the pain. On the inside, there were days I was barely pushing through, consumed by the ache of losing my babies. Some days, the weight I carried from my losses was so heavy, I just wanted to put it down. Many times I was left wondering if I would ever get to mother living children.

Deep down, I believed God had a plan. I just didn't understand why it had to include so much pain and heartache. I was trying desperately to trust Him, but between the grief of my losses and the frustration of infertility, it was hard.

Over time, I learned that grief is not just one moment. I don't just grieve the days of their deaths. I grieve all the days we didn't get to experience together. I didn't get to bake their first birthday cake. We never got to see them take their first steps or learn to ride a bike. There are always two empty chairs at the dinner table. The grief never ends. I will never get over the death of my babies.

Every loss anniversary and due date anniversary brought grief to the surface. I still struggled even after my living children were born, and the weeks leading up to May 18 continued to bring back vivid memories of the worst day of my life. Memories of the drive to the hospital, the waiting room, and being wheeled to the operating room resurfaced.

Would this day always bring such immense pain?

Drowning in Grief

After Thomas Roy and Margaret Rebecca's deaths, I reached a point where grief consumed me. I was unable to see any purpose in the immense pain I was experiencing. I had grown tired of the disappointment of staring at a negative pregnancy test each month. I was going through the motions of life, living in deep despair. The adage of "everything happens for a reason" fell short. Grief touched every aspect of my being: physically, emotionally, and spiritually. I was drowning in grief.

Living with grief day in and day out took its toll physically. This came in the form of sleepless nights, inability to focus, endless tears, and overall exhaustion. Sometimes it took every ounce of strength I had just to make it through the demands of the day, only to spend the night tossing and turning, unable to receive true rest. At work, I felt like a failure because I was unable to focus and multitask in the way my job as a teacher demanded. There were days I cried so much I didn't think I had any more tears left.

The mental and emotional impact of loss came in the form of questioning and second-guessing myself. Why was this so hard? Years after the losses, I found myself asking why it still hurt so bad. Why couldn't I just move on? There was tension as the pressure to move on was met with the realization that healing takes time. I felt hopeless as I questioned if the heaviness brought on by loss was now my "normal."

This questioning seeped into my spiritual life, too. I wondered how a good God could allow so much pain. I questioned God's plan for my life. I could not understand why He would give me the deep desire to be a mother, while month after month, I still wasn't pregnant. I often returned to the turmoil of my unanswered prayer from May 2012. I wanted his heart to have already stopped beating when we went in for that last ultrasound. I wanted God, not us, to make the decision to end his life. Why didn't God take that choice away from us?

As the weeks after loss faded into months and years, God's silence was mirrored by the silence of others. I began to feel unseen in my grief. While outwardly I seemed better, I was desperate to be on the shore watching the waves instead of drowning in them. Society seems to place a timeline on grief, and I was well past the allotted time for grieving unborn babies.

I especially felt alone on holidays. Mother's Day was the worst of them. Since I carried my children in my heart and none in my arms, my motherhood went vastly unrecognized. Why was I less of a mother, or not considered a mother at all, because my babies died? I felt overlooked and undervalued.

I felt like this storm of grief had thrown me overboard. I had to remember who was in the boat with me. I had to stop suppressing my grief and realize that acknowledging grief is holy work. The effects of holding it all in showed up through anxiety, loneliness, and hopelessness. Suppressing my grief wasn't worth the cost.

I grabbed the hand of Jesus so He could pull me aboard and help me reach the shore. My grief mattered because the love I had for my children mattered. And yours does, too.

When the World Moves On, But You Can't

I returned to work a few days after Thomas Roy died. I had used up all of my sick days and reached the point where any days missed were being deducted from my paycheck. At that time, I was a teacher, and there were only a few weeks left in the school year. I thought I could handle it.

I didn't handle it well. It was extremely difficult to resume regular activities when my world was still shaken. It took all the will and energy I had to get out of bed each morning, get myself ready, and make the forty-minute drive into work. Well-meaning co-workers shared how they had also experienced miscarriage. All I could think was that I didn't have a miscarriage. An impossible choice had to be made. We decided to end our baby's life. This felt worse than having a miscarriage. All I could think about was my dead baby as I held in my tears until the work day was over.

The arrival of summer break did not help. I was forced to resume all of the regular things like grocery shopping, paying bills, and cooking dinner. We tried to do normal things like attending a baseball game with friends, going to a concert, and taking an anniversary trip to the mountains. Over the next few months, it felt as though the world moved on while I remained stuck in grief, shock, heartbreak, deep sorrow, and despair. Grief walked with me everywhere I went.

I felt alone and unseen as I watched everyone else living their lives seemingly free of the pain I was experiencing. The deluge of sympathy cards had stopped arriving in the mailbox, and people stopped asking how I was doing. I know now I wasn't alone, unseen, or forgotten. People either didn't know what to say or they knew there was nothing to be said that could make the situation bearable.

The contrast between watching life proceed on the outside and my internal struggle was stark. I felt an unspoken pressure to move on. As time passed, I knew I needed to move forward. I wanted to move forward. But I worried that moving forward and healing meant forgetting my baby.

I read books on grief and pregnancy loss (although there were few at the time) and relied on scripture to get me through the days. Over time, I was able to see that healing is not the same as forgetting. Moving forward in grief and living life did not invalidate what was lost. Remembering is an important part of healing. Though his life was short, my baby would always be a part of mine.

A Biblical Example of Acknowledging Grief and Feeling the Pain: David's Lament

We can look at the life of David and his psalms of lament for a biblical perspective on acknowledging grief and feeling the pain of loss. Even though David was chosen by God to lead Israel, he spent years fleeing from King Saul and fearing for his life. He experienced the highest of highs as well as the lowest of lows. David was not a stranger to sorrow throughout his life, including the sorrow that comes from losing children. Many of the psalms attributed to David are psalms of lament.

Through his lament, David brought everything to God. He was not afraid to bring all of his emotions to the Lord. In the psalms, we see cries of desperation, questioning, and shameless tears. We are given an example of how to grieve in relationship with God. David shows us that grief doesn't disqualify us from a faithful life; grief is part of a faithful life. We can look at the psalms as our permission slips to question and lament without guilt.

In her book *Life Can Be Good Again*, Lisa Appelo describes lament as "voicing your hardest emotions and questions to God, leaving them there, and choosing to trust God's comfort and faithfulness."[4] Mark Vroegop defines lament as "the honest cry of a hurting heart wrestling with the paradox of pain and the promise of God's goodness."[5] Lamenting isn't merely bearing our sorrows. It is a way we can be honest with God and grieve with hope.

How can we use lament as we walk through grief? David provides an example of lament in Psalm 13 as he moves from grief and questioning to trust and hope. While this psalm moves quickly from grief to hope, it is likely only capturing a moment of David's lament. Processing grief is a process that does not happen quickly. As Psalm 13 acknowledges, it takes time:

How long, O LORD? Will you forget me forever?
How long will you hide your face from me?
How long must I take counsel in my soul
and have sorrow in my heart all the day?
How long shall my enemy be exalted over me?
Consider and answer me, O LORD my God;
light up my eyes, lest I sleep the sleep of death,
lest my enemy say, "I have prevailed over him,"
lest my foes rejoice because I am shaken.

But I have trusted in your steadfast love;
my heart shall rejoice in your salvation.
I will sing to the LORD,
because he has dealt bountifully with me. (Psalm 13)

He shows his weariness in grief as he opens with four questions that all begin by asking, "How long?" He does not hide the ongoing sorrow and feelings of abandonment he is experiencing. David moves from questioning to pleading. He turns to God, knowing He is the only one who can pull him from the darkness. In verse 3, David's despair is so deep that he would rather die than continue in the darkness. Yet, even in the darkness, he calls out to God without hiding the depth of his despair. David closes the psalm by expressing his trust that God will bring him through. This does not take his grief away; rather, it shows that faith can exist alongside our sorrow. Through his lament, David shows we can trust and praise God, even when we are brokenhearted.

Psalms of lament show us that we can cry out to God in our sorrow, even when our sorrow is so deep that we don't think we can keep going.

The Shift: I Didn't Die

Grief lingered in the aftermath of losing Thomas Roy, and later losing Margaret Rebecca. But grief wasn't the only thing that lingered. Hope was still stirring deep within.

For years, I filled pages upon pages of my journals asking how long the pain of losing my first two babies would last. How long would the impending loss anniversaries and due date anniversaries unravel me? Then, one year, as May 18 approached, God put a new song in my heart surrounding that day in 2012 when my world stopped turning. I gained a new perspective that has helped me move forward with my grief. Yes, this is the day my son died, but it is also the day I DIDN'T die.

I didn't die.

I lived through the darkness.

It still hurts to think about the life I didn't get to know.

It still hurts to think about the impossible choice we had to make.

It still hurts that he is not here—that she is not here.

A piece of my heart is still missing.

But I didn't die. I lived through my most challenging days.

There is hope—an eternal hope, an unwavering hope.

There is a trust that God knows what He is doing. There is belief in the victory that Jesus has already won.

I didn't die. I lived so that I could give life and speak life and shine His light in the darkest places.

I didn't die because my story wasn't going to end in sorrow.

Letting the Pain Speak

As humans, we often shy away from topics like pain, grief, and sorrow. When others ask how we are doing, more times than not, we reply with "I'm fine," or "Doing well." The question is asked out of social nicety, and few want to hear much more than a short reply. There is societal pressure to be okay after loss, to recover quickly, to get over it and move on. This often leads to faking it. We give the fake smile and reply: "I'm doing alright."

As Christians, we may even feel an added pressure to be strong when grieving. Putting a voice to our pain and sorrow may be seen as weakness and unbelief in a good God. Remember that Matthew 5:4 states, "Blessed are those who mourn, for they will be comforted."

Pretending to be okay is not healing. It is silencing our pain. Suppressing grief eventually has negative effects on us physically and emotionally. Elizabeth Sadock, Ph.D., says, "When we suppress unwanted emotions, we inadvertently shut off our access to positive emotions. It's like having a dimmer switch connected to all the lights in the house: When we try to dim negative emotions, all emotions become muted."[6] Sophia Dembling reveals that holding in our negative emotions can lead to apathy or depression. Grief shows up physically in many ways. It can zap energy, disrupt sleep, suppress appetites, and wreak havoc on the immune system.[7] God created all of us—mind, body, and spirit. Ignoring our emotions also affects our ability to connect with Him.

In my rush to get "back to normal" after Thomas Roy died, I began to suppress how I was really feeling. I recall unloading on a friend with the truth of how I was feeling in response to the question "How are you?" The text came through about six months after he died, and I was tired of pretending to be okay. The physical and emotional toll of holding it all inside had become more than I could take. So I told her everything. Even though she did not offer a response to my pain that made it better or made it go away, sharing how I really felt was freeing.

It is important to remember that acknowledging your pain is not a sign of weakness or defeat. Giving a voice to your grief is taking a step toward healing. It is okay to cry. It's okay to not be okay. It's also okay to still hurt, even years after the loss occurred. Where there is deep grief, there is also deep love. Acknowledging pain and voicing grief is an important step in the journey to the abundant life God has for you.

The Abundant Path: Letting Grief Speak

Grief does not need to be hidden or silent to be healed. The purpose of these steps is to help you name your pain, not fix it or make it disappear. Remember not to view these steps as a checklist to be completed. Let these suggestions guide you in giving grief a voice.

Name What You're Tired of Hiding

Think about the grief you are experiencing that no one sees. What moments do you grieve that go unseen by others? Think beyond loss anniversaries and due date anniversaries. It could be the first day of school, or a milestone birthday, or everyday moments like visiting the park. List these moments in your journal. Remember that naming your pain is not wallowing in it. Naming your hidden pain is honoring what was lost.

Pray a Psalm of Lament

Use lament as a form of prayer and a way to connect with God. Choose a psalm of lament from the suggestions below. Read it slowly as you let the words sink into your mind and heart. As you pray the scripture, be attentive to what the Holy Spirit may be speaking to you through the psalm.

Suggested psalms: Psalm 3, Psalm 6, Psalm 13, Psalm 22, Psalm 42, Psalm 44, Psalm 77, Psalm 86

Write Your Own Lament

Remember that lament is a form of faith. It can be helpful to write your own lament specific to the grief and pain you are feeling. Begin your lament by stating your hidden pain. Next, leave your plea to God. End your lament by turning to a posture of trust in Him.

Begin a Daily Ritual to Honor Your Grief

Create a daily rhythm for grief in your life. This should be a simple and tangible practice to acknowledge your ongoing grief. This small acknowledgement will not fix or eliminate your grief, nor is it intended to keep you stuck in grief. It is a way to hold space for your grief and avoid suppressing it. Here are some suggestions:

- Light a candle
- Take a walk
- Pray a psalm
- Keep a "one line a day" journal to record your pain
- Wear a piece of memorial jewelry

Share the Story You've Been Holding

Release hidden grief by speaking or writing your story. Releasing your grief in this way will help you avoid the effects of suppressing your pain. Some options for sharing are writing your story in a journal, telling a trusted friend, recording a voice memo, creating artwork that represents your grief, or writing a poem expressing your pain. Keep in mind that even if it is messy or unfinished, your story is sacred.

Let the Tears Fall

Crying is a normal emotional expression that is an important part of healing. Crying helps regulate emotions and activates the parasympathetic nervous system, which aids in recovering from stress. Tears serve as a natural pain reliever and help eliminate toxins.[8] Tears that come years after loss are not an indication of being stuck or not healing. Our tears serve as an expression of the deep love we hold for the babies we have lost. Psalm 56:8 reminds us that God keeps record of our tears. They do not go unnoticed, even if we cry in isolation. If you have been holding in your tears, find a quiet place by yourself and release what you have been holding in by letting the tears fall.

Affirm the Strength in Surviving

Even if you feel broken, you are still here. You are showing up, and that deserves to be acknowledged. Recognize your resilience by saying these words out loud: I have lived through my hardest days. Repeat these words as often as you need, especially on days when your grief feels too heavy to bear. You have walked through sorrow that many can't imagine. It's okay to give yourself credit for making it through another day.

Seek Shelter, Not Solutions

We were not meant to grieve in isolation. You need a safe space to express your grief freely without someone attempting to fix it. Find a person, group, or community that will be present in your pain, listen to your lament, and not rush the healing process. Look for presence over quick fixes and unhelpful advice.

Healing doesn't begin when pain ends. Acknowledging the pain is a step toward healing. Your sorrow may never fully go away, but it doesn't have to be hidden. God is not afraid of our tears, questions, or weariness. He wants us to bring it all to Him and lay it down at His feet. Grief may remain a part of your journey. While sorrow remains, it can join hands with joy as you learn to live abundantly after loss.

What would it look like if you let your pain speak today?

Part Two:
Finding Redemption—
Reframing Loss and Hope

CHAPTER 4

Reframing Grief

"Behold, I am doing a new thing; now it springs forth, do you not perceive it? I will make a way in the wilderness and rivers in the desert." – Isaiah 43:19

I have relived May 18, 2012, over and over in my head too many times to count. It's the day, months later, that I wished I had died. It left me asking, "Is this really my life?" This day brought so much pain. It also changed my life forever. It's the day my baby died.

Every year, when the month of May rolls around, I feel it in the pit of my stomach. It's coming—the loss anniversary. Usually, anniversaries bring memories of happy times. But not a loss anniversary. A loss anniversary brings memories of the worst time. And no matter how hard I've tried over the years to ease the blow, it hits me in the gut every time.

Memories flood my mind. Memories of pulling over on the side of the road on the way to the hospital because I was sick. Waiting in the hospital waiting room with tears streaming down my face. The sandpaper-like texture of the tissues they gave me as I waited to be rolled back to the operating room. Worrying that my husband had not had anything to eat all day. Crying as they wheeled me into the operating room. Apologizing to my baby because I couldn't save him. Waking up and telling the nurse in the recovery room that my heart hurt.

For many years, May 18 was nothing but a marker of loss. It was a day I dreaded. It took more than it gave. But at some point—through time, through faith, and through the exhaustion of carrying the weight of it all—I realized I had a choice. I could keep letting that day crush me, or I could find a way to see this horrible day differently.

Sometimes we have to redefine something, not so we can move on from it, forget it, or get over it, but so we can get through it. We have to reframe it so we can live the abundant life God has for us. Reframing loss doesn't erase the pain. It doesn't mean pretending the loss didn't happen. It simply means choosing to see the whole picture, not just the broken pieces.

Yes, May 18 will always be the day my baby died. But now, I also see it as the day that changed me. A day that reminds me where I have been, but also how far I have come. A day that, no matter how painful, holds a thread of redemption.

I'll never forget. I don't want to forget. But I can decide that this day doesn't get to define me—it gets to shape me. And in that, I find something I never thought I would: a way to live beyond the sorrow.

From Just Surviving towards Living Abundantly

For a long time, I felt like I was just existing. I was doing what I had to do to get through each day. I carried the weight of grief and could not see past it. I believed in God's promises but was unsure of how to step into them. Even after my dream of mothering living children had been realized, I was merely surviving. I wasn't living the abundant life God had for me.

I longed for more. I knew God had more in store for me, but I did not know how to move forward. I was promised abundant life in Christ, but I was missing it. I was supposed to feel full. Instead, I felt empty. When I searched the Scriptures, it was clearly written in John 10:10, "The thief comes only to steal and kill and destroy. I came that they may have life and have it abundantly."

The aftermath of loss and the grief it brings threatens to steal our joy. For so many years, I felt like grief had stolen my life. When you are in survival mode, it is hard to see past the pain. An abundant life is unimaginable. It feels unattainable.

This verse reminds us that loss is not the end of our story. Yes, grief is a thief. It steals from us. It robs us of what we should have had and the joy we should have known. It lies to us and tells us this pain will last forever. It tells us nothing good can come from our trials. I believed these lies for so long. But Jesus came so that we could have life—and not just any life but an abundant one.

I remember sitting in a hotel conference room at a writing conference many years ago and feeling the shift from survival to living in abundance begin. The workshop was on the armor of God. As the presentation drew to an end, the speakers gave participants the opportunity to be anointed with oil and have a moment of prayer with them. I waited my turn as worship music played and the prayers of faithful women filled the room.

Something inside my soul started to stir, and the Holy Spirit began speaking to me. I turned to a blank page in the conference program as the words started to flow faster than I could process them. At that moment, God was showing me a way forward. I wrote about how the things that had happened to me did not define me. I didn't have to keep reliving the most painful days. Moving forward did not mean I had forgotten the babies I had lost. I could remember them and embrace the abundant life God wanted me to have.

While I would still wrestle with this coexistence of joy and sorrow for several years, this was the beginning of seeing that God had more for me. He had a purpose in the pain.

Seeing Pain Differently

Reframing grief didn't happen for me in a single, defining moment. I didn't wake up one day and declare, "Today, I'm going to see my pain differently." It happened slowly. I spent years learning how to see how my pain could be purposeful. My thoughts gradually shifted from how badly it hurt to how I could let God use the pain for my good and His glory. It took many quiet realizations and some painful wrestling with God to get to this place.

Grief not only takes the people we love, but it takes parts of us, too. Early in my grief journey, I realized that I would never be the same person I was on May 6, 2012, the day before we received the fatal diagnosis of our first baby. That realization felt crippling. I wasn't just grieving the loss of my child; I was grieving the loss of the version of myself that existed before the loss. She didn't know this pain. She was the one who still believed life would unfold as planned. She was innocent, if even a bit naive. At times, I was angry at the loss and how much had been stolen from me. I wanted the old me back, but that wasn't going to happen.

Over time, I began to see something I never anticipated: the fact that I was a different person after loss wasn't a bad thing. The day I learned my child wouldn't live was one of the worst days of my life. Yet, in that desolation, God was working. I couldn't see it yet, but He was drawing me closer to Him. My son's death gave me a stronger faith that includes a personal relationship with Christ that had been lacking most of my adult life. I gained an eternal perspective that caused me to see the world differently. The tragedy of losing my child taught me empathy for others and gave me a greater appreciation of the people in my life.

Even though I came to see this change as a good thing, it didn't take away the grief. The sorrow still sat heavy. Some days, I could see healing on the horizon. Other days, I felt completely stuck. I was unable to move forward under the weight of loss. I knew I could not stay in this state forever. I had to find a way to a full, abundant life. But how?

I needed to reframe my grief and change my perspective on the worst day of my life. Reframing grief isn't about forgetting the loss happened or minimizing the pain. It is about deepening our perspective to see how pain can be purposeful. If we choose to, we can allow God to use our most painful moments.

Understanding that God can take our deepest pain and work it for good is a hard and powerful truth to learn. Romans 8:28 says, "And we know that for those who love God all things work together for good, for those who are called according to his purpose." We rarely see the good right away. At first, I could only see all I had lost.

Little by little, God revealed something deeper: the good wasn't in the loss itself, but in what He was doing in me through it. My pain wasn't wasted. Neither was my child's life.

Pain as a Pathway to Growth

For so long, I believed pain was something to survive. It was a season to get through so real life could begin again. I thought living in abundance would come once I moved past the grief, and it no longer had a hold on me. What if pain isn't something to just endure? What if, rather than being a barrier, it can be the thing that leads us to the abundant life Jesus' death and resurrection made possible for us? God doesn't waste our pain. He uses it to shape us.

When I look back, I can see how losing my son and all the grief that followed from a subsequent loss and struggles with infertility forced me to take a look at my faith in ways that I never had before. I truly wrestled with my faith. The surface-level truths that had gotten me through life thus far weren't good enough anymore. Easy answers didn't cut it. Not only was I asking, "Why did this happen?" I was asking, "Are you really a good God? Do you really see me? Can I trust you with this pain?"

I needed to know that even in my deepest sorrow, God was truly good. I needed more than just words. I needed an encounter with the God who promised to be near the brokenhearted. In this wrestling and searching, I developed a relationship with Christ that was more personal and intimate than ever before. While this isn't the path I would have chosen, it led me to a deeper connection with my Savior, and, in turn, produced a deeper faith within me.

A Biblical Example of Pain as a Pathway: Joseph

We can look at the life of Joseph to see how pain can be a pathway to abundant life. He was betrayed by his very own brothers, who sold him into slavery out of jealousy. He gained favor in Potiphar's house, only to be falsely accused by Potiphar's wife and unjustly imprisoned. He was forgotten in prison by the Pharaoh's cupbearer. Joseph spent years suffering before he saw any redemption. His situation seemed unfair and unending, just like our grief often does. He could have easily become bitter, lost faith, and given up, yet he continued to trust God.

Just as we often can't see purpose in our pain in the moment, Joseph couldn't see how God was using his suffering while he was in it. However, every hardship he endured was preparing him for what was to come. Joseph's suffering positioned him to interpret Pharaoh's dreams, save Egypt from famine, and rescue his family. In Genesis 50:20, he acknowledges that God used his suffering to accomplish something greater: "As for you, you meant evil against me, but God meant it for good, to bring it about that many people should be kept alive, as they are today."

As he sat in prison, Joseph didn't know he would save an entire nation one day. He did not see how every betrayal, every hardship, was positioning him for something greater. We don't see that in our own suffering either—at least not at first. What if, like Joseph, our pain is positioning us for something greater than we can even imagine? What if God is orchestrating our redemption in the very moments we feel forgotten?

For a long time, I believed that abundant life meant a life free of sorrow. Healing meant moving past grief, as if one day, the pain would just fade away. I have learned that sorrow and joy coexist. Grief doesn't disappear. It becomes woven into who we are. Even when sorrow is still present, God invites us to experience joy. This is not a joy that replaces the pain. It is a joy that sits beside it. We're not leaving grief behind. We're not moving on. We're moving forward and trusting that joy and sorrow can share the same space.

I won't pretend this journey is easy. And I do not have all the answers. I do know this—God does not waste pain, and He's not asking us to pretend this great loss doesn't hurt. He is asking us to trust that He can use the worst thing that ever happened to us. He will use it to lead us to something greater if we let Him. It can lead to healing, purpose, and a life of abundance. It will never look like we expected, but it will be exactly what He intended.

James 1 has been a guidepost for me throughout my path to abundant living after loss. In verses 2-4, we are encouraged to look beyond the pain to something greater: "Count it all joy, my brothers, when you meet trials of various kinds, for you know that the testing of your faith produces steadfastness. And let steadfastness have its full effect, that you may be perfect and complete, lacking in nothing."

When Grief Walks Beside You

I understand how difficult it is to believe that an abundant life is possible after loss. When grief feels overwhelming, the abundant life God has for you seems like it was meant for other people but not for you. I get it. I've been there.

There was a time when I couldn't imagine life feeling anything but heavy. I didn't have all the answers, and I certainly didn't feel ready for anything that resembled abundance. I wasn't sure how to step into the promises of God when my heart was still broken. But even then, something in me knew I couldn't stay where I was.

Many people think grief will fade over time. I've learned that grief doesn't go away. Grief changes. She becomes a steady presence in our lives after loss, changing positions but never disappearing. For a long time, grief stood directly in front of me, blocking the way forward. Then she moved beside me, not blocking my way forward, but still present. Eventually, as I began to reframe my loss, she moved behind me. She didn't disappear. She was still part of my story, but she no longer had control. Even now, she sometimes sneaks up beside me or in front of me, reminding me that grief is never truly gone, just repositioned, reframed.

Living an abundant life doesn't mean I'm happy all the time. It doesn't mean I've forgotten. My grief hasn't vanished. Instead, I've learned to hold joy and sorrow together. I've learned to believe that God still has goodness for me, even when life looks nothing like I thought it would.

There were days I could barely get out of bed, let alone imagine purpose in my pain. Over time, I started to notice small things, glimpses of grace that didn't erase the ache but softened it. A kind word. A sunrise. The way someone looked me in the eye and said my baby's name. These weren't steps in a process. They were sacred invitations to look again.

I eventually realized I didn't have to choose between grief and gratitude. I could be heartbroken and thankful. I could cry and still believe in goodness. And maybe, just maybe, I could live a full life not in spite of my loss, but because of what God was doing through it.

Even now, I'm still figuring it out. Some days, I trust easily. Other days, I wrestle with all the questions I thought I'd already let go. But I know this: God isn't waiting for me to get over my grief before He offers me abundant life. He's offering it right here in the middle of the pain.

What if you laid your sorrow in God's hands instead of holding it alone? What if you were open to letting God reframe your grief? What if your pain could be a pathway to abundant life? What if that abundant life isn't waiting at the end of your healing, but is already unfolding?

God doesn't waste anything. Not your tears or your loss or your story.

The Abundant Path: Reframing Grief

Reframing grief isn't something that happens all at once. It's a process. It is a choice we make over and over to see our pain through a different lens. Grief doesn't disappear. We don't wake up one day all of a sudden free from its weight. The grief stays, but we can choose how we carry it. We can stay stuck, or we can let God use our pain to help shape us and lead us forward.

Grief changes us. It will always be a part of our story, but it doesn't have to be the whole story. Reframing grief means learning to hold sorrow and joy together while trusting that God is working in the brokenness. It's not about moving on; it's about moving forward. It's about believing that living an abundant life isn't about forgetting the past but learning to live fully while carrying the weight of loss.

I know this isn't easy. I also know it's possible. If you're wondering where to start, here are some next steps to help you on your journey.

Commit to One Small Step Forward

Ask yourself: What is one small way I can reframe my grief today, enabling it to shape me rather than weigh me down?

Make this simple, and remember this is a journey. Start small.

- Write down one thing you're grateful for.
- Spend a few moments in prayer and surrender your grief to God.
- Reach out to someone and share part of your story.
- Take a walk and notice signs of life and the beauty around you.

Practice Reframing Your Grief

Try this reflection exercise. Write down a painful moment that still weighs heavily on you. Create two columns: on the left side, write "What I Lost," and on the right side, write "What This Loss Has Taught Me/How God Has Used It."

Ask yourself: How has this pain shaped me? What have I learned through it? How might God be using this for something greater?

Identify and Celebrate Small Moments of Abundance

Start an "Abundance Journal." Intentionally look for one moment of goodness or grace every day. This could be a moment of peace, a conversation that uplifts you or brings you comfort, or simply the presence of someone who cares. Even if this moment feels small, write it down.

Ask yourself: What if abundance doesn't mean the absence of pain? What if abundance is the presence of God's goodness in the midst of pain? How can these small moments of goodness and grace help me reframe my grief?

Embrace Joy Without Guilt

Allowing yourself to feel joy again is one of the hardest parts of grieving. It can feel like a betrayal of your loss, but it isn't a betrayal. Give yourself permission to experience joy without feeling guilty. Remind yourself that choosing joy does not mean forgetting your loss. It means you're still living—and that's okay.

Ask yourself: Would my baby want me to live in sorrow forever? Is grief the only way to honor my baby's memory? Can I honor my baby by living fully? How can embracing joy help me carry on my baby's memory in a way that honors my love for them?

Lean Into God's Presence Every Day

Start (or strengthen) your prayer practice. Even when you don't have the words, sit in God's presence and let Him meet you there.

When you don't know what to pray, start here: "Dear God, I don't know what to say and I don't understand this, but I'm here. Meet me in my grief."

Read and meditate on Scripture. Here are some passages that can remind you of God's faithfulness:

- Psalm 23
- Isaiah 61:3
- Romans 8:28

Ask yourself: How can I create space in my day to be present with God? Am I being honest with God about my grief, or am I holding back? What would it look like to invite God into my pain instead of carrying it alone?

Find Ways to Use Your Story for Good

Remember that your pain doesn't disqualify you from doing good. Your pain equips you. God can use it for good if you let Him.

Ask yourself: How has my pain uniquely prepared me to offer something meaningful to others? Could I write about my experience? Could I be a listening ear to someone experiencing a similar loss? Could I participate in a grief support group or similar ministry?

Choose Trust Over Understanding

Make a conscious effort to trust God with the parts of your story you don't yet understand. When you have doubt, remind yourself that God sees the full picture and you don't have to understand it to trust Him.

Ask yourself: What unanswered questions about my loss am I still holding onto? How can I begin to surrender them to God? How has God been faithful to me before? How can remembering his past faithfulness help me trust him with what I don't understand now?

You don't have to figure it all out today. Just take one step— just one small step to start reframing your grief. God isn't waiting for you to move on from your grief before giving you the abundant life made possible through the death and resurrection of His Son. He's offering you that abundant life right now in the middle of your pain. Trust Him with your sorrow and watch Him create something beautiful.

CHAPTER 5

Embodied Grief, Sacred Healing

"My flesh and my heart may fail, but God is the strength of my heart and my portion forever." —Psalm 73:26

As I came out of anesthesia in the recovery room, I tearfully muttered, "My heart hurts." Earlier that day, I walked into the hospital with a dying baby in my womb. Hours later, I was leaving with an empty womb and a shattered heart. "Your heart will heal," the nurse whispered in my ear as she wheeled me into the elevator.

In the years that followed, I waited for healing. I waited for the gaping holes in my heart not to hurt so badly. I waited for the triggers to stop being triggers. I waited, but my heart still hurt. The emptiness that filled my heart that May day remained. I was still broken. My heart wasn't healed.

The nurse said my heart would heal, but I eventually came to learn that healing did not mean the pain of losing my children would disappear. For me, healing was not the absence of pain. It did not come tied up with a pretty red bow, making everything better. Healing was messy.

The holes left in my heart by the two babies I lost are always going to hurt, and at times, just as badly as the initial pain of losing them. Triggers will always be present, although their intensity may fade. When I look at my family, two will always be missing.

I came to believe God leaves us a little broken so we will always lean on His strength. We would not need His presence in our lives if we were completely healed and whole. Jesus died on the cross so we can receive complete healing when we enter into eternity with Him.

My heart didn't heal the way I thought it would. When my life after loss journey began, I thought healing meant the pain caused by the losses would eventually go away. I was wrong. The sorrow I endured after losing Thomas Roy and, later, Margaret Rebecca, remained.

Living with such a significant loss did not get any easier over time. I had to choose to embrace a new normal. I chose to let God bind up my wounds and hold them as I journey through my life here. I let my loss make me a better person and give me a greater purpose.

Grief Embodied

When I began this journey of grief, I didn't realize that grief isn't just something I feel emotionally. I thought healing only involved learning to live with the losses. The brokenness I experienced wasn't only spiritual and emotional; it was also physical. I didn't realize my body was holding on to the grief—that my body carries grief just as deeply as my heart.

Over the years, I have learned that my body always knows grief is coming before my heart and my mind. I know the months of May, June, November, and February will bring grief. These months hold the death anniversaries and the due date anniversaries of my first two babies. The grief often shows up physically before I'm mentally and emotionally aware that it is there.

My patience with others grows thin. Anxiety sneaks in, and I feel it in the pit of my stomach. I get overwhelmed and overstimulated more quickly than usual. I'm exhausted, but I have trouble sleeping. My chest feels heavy. A sense of doom settles in before I realize what is happening. Then my mind catches up. I check the calendar and see the impending marker of grief approaching. A tension develops between trying to stay busy to ignore the coming pain and the need to work through it.

Lauren Sillis explains that even though grief is an emotion, it also has physical manifestations. If we do not find a way to work through our grief, it will show up in our physical bodies. Physical manifestations of grief can include sleep disturbances, digestive issues, headaches, hypertension, and heart disease, just to name a few.[9] Unprocessed grief can bring dire consequences.

Time has taught me a variety of ways to process and move through these expected moments of grief. When grief manifests itself physically, and I realize what is happening, I have to find God in my pain. Three ways I have learned to rely on to move through these moments are through nature, movement, and music. These pathways help me encounter God and tend to the weight of grief on my body and mind.

Creation as Comfort

Spending time in nature, the part of our world created by God, has played an important role in how I move through grief. Whether it's watching the sunrise, sitting by water, or looking over a mountain peak, I feel most connected with my Creator while experiencing His creation. This connection began early on in my grief journey.

The weekend before we received Thomas Roy's fatal diagnosis was full of worry and fear. We knew something was wrong, but we did not know the extent of the issues. I was so scared. As I was driving through a torrential downpour, I decided to pull over and wait out the storm. I do this often, as I hate driving in the rain. As the storm cleared, I looked up to see the most beautiful rainbow. I was brought to tears as I looked at the vivid colors that filled the sky and was reminded of God's promises. For a brief moment, I was able to lay down my anxiety over the unknown and experience a peace beyond my understanding.

Since that day, I have often found myself looking up through my journey of healing. The sunrise, a blue sky filled with white, puffy clouds, and the sunset started to catch my attention. The colors God painted in the sky captivated me. I found myself drawn to spend more time in nature. I began to find solace in sitting on my swing in the yard with a hot mug of coffee as I watched and listened to the world wake up.

Chasing sunrises and sunsets became healing for me. Looking at the beautiful picture God paints in the sky each morning and listening to the birds chirping and roosters crowing as the world wakes up brings me peace and helps me feel closer to my Creator.

When grief is heavy, I am drawn to the wide open spaces of creation. One special place God has met me in my grief is Fred W.

Symmes Chapel. This open-air chapel, also called Pretty Place, is located on the edge of a cliff in the upstate of South Carolina near the North Carolina border. The stone altar that features a large wooden cross in the center looks out on the Blue Ridge Mountains. It's beautiful any time of day, but the beauty of a sunrise at Pretty Place is breathtaking.

As what should have been Thomas Roy's fifth birthday approached, I felt drawn to experience a Pretty Place sunrise to mark the day. Living with the pain of losing him and Margaret Rebecca was still hard, despite much healing and the fulfillment of mothering my two living children. On November 19, 2017, Keith and I woke up early to make the two-hour drive. We arrived in the darkness and found a seat on one of the wooden benches. As the sky turned from dark to light, and the beautiful red, orange, and yellow hues filled the sky, I sat with my head on his shoulder with tears rolling down my face.

Another part of God's creation where I feel closer to Him is the ocean. Standing on the shoreline looking out at the vast expanse of water always leaves me in awe. The ebb and flow of the waves is synonymous with the grief that comes with life after loss.

We went on a beach trip for my 34th birthday, a few months after Thomas Roy died. I remember sitting in the sand watching the sun rise on a birthday I didn't feel like celebrating. Watching the sun peek up from the horizon as the waves went in and out brought an immense peace that surpassed all understanding during a time when my grief was still very new and raw.

Since that time, I have always tried to take in a beach sunrise whenever I am near the ocean. Listening to the crashing waves as the sun rises on another day is a reminder that God is in control and His mercies are new every morning. It's a powerful reassurance that even in the pain, everything will be okay.

Mark Brewer stresses that spending time in nature can have psychological and physical benefits. Being in nature can help calm the mind and reduce anxiety, depression, and stress. When we are exposed to natural sunlight, vitamin D levels, which are important for our immune systems, increase. Observing the natural processes of growth and renewal can provide hope.[10]

All of these moments in nature, both big and small, help ground me. They remind me of how big and wide this wonderful world is and how big and wide the Creator's love is for me. When grief is heavy and sorrow sneaks in, I find comfort in creation and in knowing that the God who made the universe loves me and wants the best for me.

Carrying Heavy

After my daughter was born in 2016, I decided to start taking my physical health more seriously. I began eating better and exercising regularly. Physical movement can help process grief and has many benefits. Dave DePew explains that exercise causes the body to release endorphins, which help elevate our mood. It can also help calm the nervous system and help move us out of the "fight or flight" response to grief. Moving our bodies has also been shown to improve sleep quality.[11]

My movement journey began with a workout DVD, and months later, it turned into training for a 5K. I completed my first 5K in November 2016. During my training, I developed a love for working out outside in nature. We purchased a double stroller that I used to push around while walking and jogging.

During the period when I began walking, jogging, and running more, my husband was introduced to rucking through his workout group, F3. Rucking has military roots and involves carrying weight on your back while walking. When Keith started rucking with his F3 friends, I thought it was a little strange. When he decided to participate in a GORUCK endurance event, I thought he was downright crazy.

A GORUCK event involves more than just rucking. These team events are led by Cadre, who are former Special Forces. During the event, which lasts anywhere from six to twenty-four hours, participants carry their rucksacks, as well as sandbags and other heavy items, over many miles. They learn to work as a team as the Cadre presents various physical and mental challenges.

One day in January 2018, I decided to find out for myself what rucking was all about. I wrapped a towel around a dumbbell and threw it into an old backpack that had once been used as a diaper bag before our daily walk. I never stopped rucking after that day. A few months later, Keith and I carried our toddlers in child carrier backpacks over the Arthur Ravenel, Jr. Bridge in the Cooper River Bridge Run, a 10K race held annually in Charleston, South Carolina. Then I completed my first of many GORUCK events in September 2018.

Some of the most meaningful GORUCK events I have completed are the all-female events held annually in various parts of the country. I have participated in these in Louisville, KY, Austin, TX, and Nashville, TN. There's something unique about a group of women coming together to accomplish hard things.

After my losses, my struggles to become pregnant, and my fight with endometriosis, I felt like my body had failed me. Participating in these events and carrying the heavy weight, conquering the physical challenges presented, felt like fighting back. The heaviness of the ruck, sandback, logs, and whatever else we were asked to carry was the physical embodiment of the weight of the grief I carried. Rucking became an outlet for moving forward in the aftermath of grief. The endurance events served as a mirror to my grief journey.

Signing up for these events is the easy part. Showing up is the hard part. There are always obstacles to face when training for and participating in events. As a wife and mom, my biggest obstacle was the time training and events took away from my family. Where would the kids stay while Keith was at work? Can we afford the expenses associated with an out-of-state event? Am I physically prepared to complete the event?

Hearing a doctor say, "It's not good," was not the hardest part of my grief journey. Neither was making the impossible decision to end my son's life. Being wheeled into the operating room with tears streaming down my face and the physical pain that followed the procedure wasn't the hardest part either. Those things were all difficult, but the hardest part of my grief journey became showing up for life after loss. Choosing to show up for my life and live it abundantly rather than just survive each day is not easy.

Every GORUCK event requires work. Some of it is physical, and a lot of it is mental. In every GORUCK event, I received help and support that enabled me to persevere and complete the challenge. Many of these amazing ladies participating in these events alongside me went out of their way to get me through. This has included coming beside me as I was struggling through bear crawls and doing them with me. Another time, I received encouragement to keep going while carrying the 80-pound sandbag with another participant. Others listened as I shared about my babies without the usual platitudes that often follow when I tell my story. The help of others is necessary to make it through these events. It's about the team.

Grief also requires work. Some of it is physical, and most of it is mental. Along the journey, many people have helped me, knowingly and unknowingly. People sent cards and visited and prayed. Other loss moms have shared their stories. There are listening ears. There are those who remember my babies and call them by name, understanding that a loss mama's deepest fear is that people will forget. Other people are necessary on the journey through grief.

I leave these events feeling refreshed, strong, and joyful with the confidence to face the challenges ahead. Every GORUCK event I have completed has left me with more confidence, which spurs me to become stronger, train harder, and try more challenging things.

Each year that passes that I choose to show up for life instead of just surviving also gives me more confidence to face difficult times head-on and fight for joy.

These events challenge me to become stronger, to be better than I was the day before, to learn, and to meet new people. They also serve as a reminder that I made it. I survived my worst day. The hell on Earth I endured did not take me down. And I didn't just survive, I chose to show up for my life and live it abundantly.

Music as Medicine

Music has played an important role in my life since childhood. I always loved to sing and participated in the chorus throughout elementary school. In the sixth grade, I joined the band and learned to play the flute. This carried through my high school and college years. I continued to play in church many years after college. I eventually put the instrument down and stopped playing.

Several years ago, my former band director, who taught me how to play the flute in sixth grade, co-founded a community wind ensemble in a neighboring town. Having not played in nearly ten years, and never having dreamed of playing in a group or publicly again, I decided to join the ensemble for its inaugural season. Since that season, I've played with the group twice a year.

Making music again has provided me with a creative outlet to process life. The joy of coming together with others and combining our talents to create beautiful sounds is life-giving. It has enabled me to reconnect with something I have loved for most of my life. Spending a couple of hours on Thursday evenings, a few months out of the year, has brought abundance to my life.

Over the years, I have also processed grief through worship music. Worshipping God through music helps bring focus back to His promises rather than my sorrow. Singing out to God prepares my heart to hear what the Spirit is saying to me.

In addition to making music, I have always enjoyed attending live music events. I rarely pass up the opportunity to see a great country music artist perform live. Going to concerts was a big part of my and Keith's dating and early married life. It started in the late '90s when we attended the George Strait Country Music Festival for many years.

After unbearable grief, it's hard to live again and participate in activities that once filled life with happiness. Just a little over a month after losing Thomas Roy, Keith and I were given tickets to see two of our favorites from our dating years—Kenny Chesney and Tim McGraw. I was excited to be there, but still hurting deeply. As

Tim McGraw sang his hit, "Live Like You Were Dying," I held back tears. The lyrics got to me, but crying in public was unfamiliar and uncomfortable for me. I felt the need to hide my tears. Having a complete breakdown in the middle of a country music concert felt weak.

Six years later, I found myself listening to the same lyrics live as Tim McGraw performed. This time, as I sang along, I didn't hold back. I let the tears flow. I learned the best thing I can do for my grief is to let the emotions come whenever, wherever, and however they come. Pushing back tears and pretending everything is okay always did more damage than good. I became okay with crying in public. This became one of the greatest displays of strength and love I can make.

There is always at least one song that reminds me of my grief and evokes a deep emotional response. It's common for tears to form several times as I'm listening to my favorite artists perform. Sometimes the teardrops stay nestled in the corner of my eyes. Other times, they stream down my face. Whether they are tears of sorrow or tears of joy, barely there or visibly evident, they serve as a poignant reminder of my full and abundant life.

Music has been used as a form of therapy since Ancient Greek times.[12] Listening to music has been shown to lower stress, decrease heart rate, and reduce pain levels. It has the ability to promote a sense of relaxation.[13] Attending live music performances has been shown to release endorphins, dopamine, and oxytocin, all of which are neural pathways commonly associated with pleasure.[14]

Whether it's making music, worshiping through music, or listening to live music, music has served as a powerful way for me to process grief and step into an abundant life.

A Biblical Example of Embodied Grief and Sacred Encounter: Jesus at Gethsemane

We find a biblical example of embodied grief and sacred encounter in Jesus' time at the Garden of Gethsemane before His crucifixion. Luke tells us Jesus often withdrew to the Mount of Olives: "And every day he was teaching in the temple, but at night he went out and lodged on the mount called Olivet" (Luke 21:37). The night before His crucifixion was no different. After administering the last supper to the disciples, He retreated to Gethsemane, located on the Mount of Olives.

Although the exact location of Gethsemane is unknown, it was situated on the Mount of Olives. Jessica Brodie reveals that we know it was an important place to Jesus, as it is referenced in all four Gospels and the book of Acts. The Greek translation of Gethsamane means "an oil press." The Garden of Gethsemane is thought to be "a small garden, plot of ground or enclosure tucked away and relatively private," and likely housed an olive press.[15]

In Matthew 26, Jesus expresses His sorrow to the disciples who were with Him. Then He "fell on his face and prayed" (Matthew 26:39). Jesus chose a quiet place in nature to withdraw and process His deep sorrow. He did not hide His grief; He brought it to His Father. He is modeling how to let our bodies carry sorrow and not deny it. This passage also illustrates how natural spaces can serve as sacred places for processing grief.

Grief shows up in Jesus' body. He falls to the ground in a state of deep sorrow. His sweat was so intense that it "became like great drops of blood falling down to the ground" (Luke 22:44). God in human form experienced the physical effects of grief just as we do.

I connect Jesus' time in the Garden of Gethsemane with my moments in nature with the Father. I have had many moments of taking my grief to God while sitting on my swing watching the sunset and sitting by the ocean watching the waves.

Jesus did not hide His grief or avoid the sorrow. He brought it to the Father, and He did so in a sacred natural space. We can also honor our grief physically and spiritually, trusting that God will meet us in it.

The Abundant Path: Honoring Grief in Body and Spirit

Grief lives in the body and spirit, and God cares for both. The steps in this section are an invitation to tend to the physical weight of sorrow and create sacred spaces to encounter God in your grief. Remember to view these not as a checklist to be completed, but gentle suggestions to help you move forward.

Create a Movement Routine

Choose an intentional way to move your body. The movement doesn't have to be complex. It can be as simple as taking a walk or stretching. Find something easy and enjoyable for you to do regularly. If you have the ability and the desire to do more, you could try rucking, running, hiking, or strength training. Approach this as a time to be present with your body, rather than escaping the pain.

Return to Nature

When sorrow feels heavy, spend some time in nature. Find a favorite spot outside. This could be a yard swing, a park bench, or a spot by the water. Set aside distractions and be still. Pay attention to what you see and hear. Think about how creation reveals God's faithfulness. Let yourself feel whatever comes.

Rest Your Body with Intention

Grief exhausts the heart, but it can also exhaust the body. Intentional rest should not be equated with laziness. It is a crucial part of the healing process. Carve out time to lie down, take a nap, or go to bed early. Rest is an act of trust as you lay down what you can't carry and let God care for you. We can withdraw to quiet places just as Jesus did.

Make a Grief Playlist

Listening to music can be a powerful pathway for healing. Create a list of songs that permit you to feel sadness and hope. If you need a starting point, refer to the list in the "Moving Forward: Tools for the Journey" section in the back of the book.

Creatively Express Your Grief

Artistic creation can be a great outlet for expressing your sorrow. Choose a simple creative outlet where you can express yourself without feeling pressured to make the art perfect or even good. You could try painting, doodling, crafting, or arranging flowers. This is a gentle way for your hands to speak what your heart is holding.

Journal with the Body in Mind

It's easy to overlook what our bodies carry. Writing things down can help process how grief presents itself and ways that are helpful in processing grief. Reflect on how your body feels after movement, being in nature, listening to music, resting intentionally, or expressing yourself creatively. Write it down. Where did you feel tension? Were there tears? Did the activity lighten or intensify anything? There's no right or wrong way to do this. Just write down what you notice and how you feel.

Healing in the way I imagined it when the nurse told me my heart would heal never happened. Grief continues to show up emotionally and physically. I have learned that God cares for all of me—mind, body, and spirit. He cares for all of you, too. When we tend to our grief emotionally, spiritually, and physically, we honor God and live abundantly.

Your healing journey may not be unfolding as you imagined, either. It's okay to feel the weight of grief as you move toward abundant life. Know that you are not alone. Keep moving forward, trusting that God meets you every step of the way.

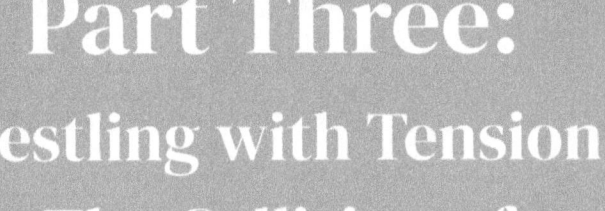

Part Three:
Wrestling with Tension—
The Collision of
Joy and Sorrow

CHAPTER 6

Parenting After Loss

"So she called the name of the Lord who spoke to her, 'You are a God of seeing,' for she said, 'Truly here I have seen him who looks after me.'" – Genesis 16:13

In late 2014, when I was pregnant with my son, we began purchasing baby furniture and setting up his room. It felt surreal. My previous pregnancies ended long before we reached this stage of preparation. Choosing and buying the crib, a changing table, and shelves to hold all the baby things was an act of hope that this pregnancy would end differently.

One of our purchases was a rocking recliner. As I sat down in the floor model at the store, I could picture it in the room and imagined myself sitting in the chair holding our newborn baby. As I sat in the chair, more pregnant than I had ever been, I wondered, "Would this time be different?" I wanted to go all in and believe it would be different, but fear always crept in, telling me I may never get the chance to hold a living child. I sat in the tension of the hope of holding a newborn and the fear that it would never happen. I leaned into hope that day as I fell in love with the light gray color and soft texture of the chair and knew we had to get it for his room.

In the weeks leading up to his birth, I would sit in the recliner and write letters to him in a journal. Part of me still didn't believe we would bring a baby home, so this journal, where I documented the final weeks of the pregnancy and told him how much I loved him, served as evidence of his life. As I sat in the chair, feeling him kick and move around inside my womb, I thought about how it would feel to finally hold him. I also thought about the two babies before him that I never got to hold. As I felt his kicks, I prayed for him to make it into my arms.

After we brought a healthy baby boy home from the hospital, I would sit in the recliner to feed him, rock him to sleep, and just hold him. It's the same recliner I sat in when I was overcome with emotion during his newborn photos. I spent countless hours in this chair with my baby.

As I held him and cared for him, I was often consumed with thoughts of all I had missed out on with my first two babies. I never got to hold them. I never got to feed or soothe them as I wiped away their tears. I never got to rock them to sleep in that chair. So many moments were stolen by their deaths.

This chair became a place where joy and sorrow intertwined, and I felt the tension of their coexistence. It was a place where I held babies both in my arms and in my heart.

Eleven months after his birth, we brought my daughter home, and this same recliner was the place where I would feed her, rock her to sleep, and just hold her. It didn't take long for my son to climb up in the chair as I cared for his sister.

Over the years, the chair became our place for cuddles and comfort, stories and singing, laughter and tears. If one child joined me in the chair, it usually wasn't long before the other climbed onto the other side of my lap. The light gray recliner made its way to different rooms in the house, yet it remained our special place.

The chair was also where I often sat alone, documenting life within the pages of my journal. I wrote about the joyful moments, and I wrote about the grief. I poured my heart out on its pages as I tried to make sense of the immense joy and sorrow I was experiencing. I was caught off guard by the mixed emotions that came from parenting after loss. Writing it all down served as a way for me to process these emotions and accept that joy and sorrow could coexist.

One ordinary day, when my kids were preschoolers, we were snuggled up in the chair together as we often did. My son and daughter were much bigger than they had been years before, and maneuvering our way into a comfortable position with all three of us in the chair was becoming more challenging. As we struggled to get comfortable, my daughter looked at me and said, "If my other brother and my sister were here, this chair would be really crowded."

I paused at her matter-of-fact declaration, imagining how holding all four of my children in that chair would feel. Joy and sorrow filled the moment as I felt tears well up and a lump form in my throat. I squeezed them tighter as I acknowledged the truth in her words.

Holding my living children in this crowded chair has brought me great joy. At times, it has magnified the pain of losing my first two babies. It has been a place of grieving and a place of healing. It has felt crowded and empty at the same time.

When Motherhood Feels Fragmented

Samuel's first birthday party was a day full of joy. I had meticulously planned out every detail amid caring for a newborn and an almost one-year-old. I dreamed of baking and decorating birthday cakes for my children for so many years. And now the time had finally come. I baked the cake and decorated it to match the airplane theme of the party. The party decorations were in place, the gifts wrapped, and the food prepared. Family and friends arrived with gifts. It was time to celebrate one year of Samuel.

While everyone sang the Happy Birthday song, I walked toward Samuel, who was perched in a wooden highchair I had borrowed for the occasion. I carried his baby sister on my chest in a baby carrier and his birthday cake in my arms. By the time I made it to the highchair and put the cake on the tray, my eyes had filled with tears. Tears of joy for a moment I had dreamed of for so long, and tears of sorrow at the realization of a moment I missed out on twice.

This is just one example of how my motherhood after loss feels fragmented, torn between what I have and what I am missing. My arms are full and empty at the same time. And my heart is whole and aching all at once.

Before my living children were born, my motherhood was defined by sorrow. I deeply loved two babies I could not hold; babies I never got the chance to hold. My identity as a mother went unacknowledged by most.

I desperately prayed for living children and often wondered if my prayers would be answered. The births of my living children were filled with joy. My prayers had been answered, and I finally held two babies in my arms.

I soon learned that mothering two children in my arms and two in my heart is not easy. The grief and sorrow I lived with after the death of my first two babies did not disappear when my living children were born. My longing to hold my babies who died did not go away after I held my babies who lived.

Being a mother to the seen and unseen brings about many emotions. There have been times I have felt guilty for feeling joy with my living children while still grieving my babies who died.

I have felt misunderstood and sometimes angry when only the seen side of my motherhood is acknowledged by others. Sometimes healing has felt scary, like a betrayal of my babies in heaven. These emotions create an internal tension no one sees.

After my daughter was born, people often commented that we had the perfect family. While these comments were well-meaning and not meant to hurt me, they always stung a little. The perception of others that we have the perfect family deeply conflicted with my internal struggle. The perfect family everyone saw was incomplete. We were missing two. We would always be missing two. And that reality is hard to reconcile.

My days were filled to the brim and empty all at the same time as I navigated this fragmented motherhood. I had to learn how to make space for the seen and the unseen. How do we make the invisible visible as we live life after loss? What does it mean to mother children here and in heaven?

Visible and Invisible Motherhood

Parenting after loss is made up of the visible and the invisible. Visible motherhood is the part the world sees. It's pushing little ones through the grocery store, park visits, and beach trips. It's the highlight reel we post on social media for everyone to see.

Invisible motherhood is the part no one sees. It's loving babies we never got to hold, grieving the life we thought we'd have, and remembering when it seems the world has forgotten. While the world mostly only affirms the visible side of motherhood, both sides are authentic and valid. They both deserve to be acknowledged.

After Samuel and Emma Joy were born, I had to figure out how to navigate these two sides of motherhood. Early on, I struggled with the tension between the two, especially around times of loss anniversaries.

During these times, the pain of the losses became paralyzing again. Every day felt like a fight to stay afloat. I questioned why the days leading up to these anniversaries were still hard and left me feeling stuck year after year.

How could I keep the worst thing that ever happened to me from bringing me down every year?

How could I remember my babies without sinking into the pit of depression?

How could I honor my babies in heaven without diminishing the joy of life now?

I struggled with these things internally while the world saw our perfect family of four enjoying life. I shied away from sharing too much about the pain of the losses for fear of being misunderstood. I worried others would perceive my remembering as being ungrateful for the blessings that came years later.

I also worried that my grief would have an adverse effect on Samuel and Emma Joy's childhood. I feared they would develop a stigma around these days because they were times Mommy changed and became really sad. In order for that not to happen, I decided to bring them into my grief.

Young children are capable of understanding far more than we give them credit for. From the moment they could understand, my children were told about the two babies who came before them. They learned that the babies died inside Mommy's womb and now live in heaven with Jesus. We talked about how life doesn't end on earth when we die, but we have eternal life in heaven if we accept Jesus's gift of forgiveness granted by His death on the cross.

We openly talked about Thomas Roy and Margaret Rebecca. My daughter often told people that her mommy has four babies, two here and two in heaven. She proudly explained that she had another brother and a sister in heaven.

Just as we were open about the losses, I tried not to hide the sadness that came from losing them. As I made memories with my living children, I found ways to remember the two babies I never got to hold.

The first Christmas after Thomas Roy died, I sponsored a child from a local Angel Tree who was the same age he would have been. I purchased clothes, toys, and books for this child that I likely would have bought for him had he lived. The following Christmas, I chose two names of children the same ages as Thomas Roy and Margaret Rebecca would have been. I did this for a few years until the symbolism became too much for me to bear.

When Samuel and Emma Joy were preschoolers, we started a Christmas Toy Drive that has become an annual tradition. We set a movement goal each year and raise money to purchase bikes that we donate to our local Toys for Tots campaign. We honor and remember our babies in heaven while helping other children's Christmas wishes come true.

I carve out time to honor and remember on due date anniversaries and death anniversaries. Sometimes, this involves all four of us. Oftentimes, I break away by myself to grieve and remember. Either way, I am open about my sadness as I take the opportunity to continue to share the hope of heaven with Samuel and Emma Joy.

On ordinary days when grief and sorrow break through moments of joy, I let the tears fall. When those tears get noticed, I share the grief behind them. I try not to hide my feelings. I want my children to see grief as a regular part of life and nothing to be ashamed of.

Living with visible and invisible motherhood is complicated, but it is also sacred. Our unseen motherhood deserves to be brought into the light. Acknowledging the pain, the grief, the longing for what we cannot hold does not negate the blessings everyone can see.

A Biblical Example of Seen and Unseen: Hagar

In the Bible, we find a mother who felt unseen and forgotten, yet God met her in her distress. Her name is Hagar, and her story is recorded in the book of Genesis. Hagar was the servant of Sarai, the wife of Abram. Sarai had been unable to bear children, so she came up with a plan to have Abram impregnate her servant Hagar. Once Hagar became pregnant with Abram's child, she began to treat Sarai with contempt, which caused Sarai to become angry and likely jealous. In return, Sarai treated Hagar so harshly that it caused Hagar to flee.

In her despair, an angel appeared to her, providing her hope in what felt like a hopeless situation. The angel told Hagar to return to Sarai and submit to her. The angel promised Hagar that the son she carried in her womb would lead a great nation. In that moment, Hagar felt seen. She called out to God in Genesis 16:13, "'You are a God of seeing,' for she said, 'Truly here I have seen him who looks after me.'" Hagar returned to Sarai and later bore a son whom she named Ishmael, as the angel had instructed her.

Years later, after God fulfilled his promise to Abraham and Sarah (formerly Abram and Sarai) by giving them a son, Sarah told Abraham to send Hagar and Ishmael away for fear Ishmael would take her son Isaac's inheritance. In Genesis 21, God shows up for Hagar and Ishmael again. In their trek through the wilderness of Beersheba, they ran out of water. Hagar put Ishmael under a bush and left him because she could not bear watching him die. She was again in a hopeless situation. She called out to God as "she lifted up her voice and wept" (Genesis 21:16).

An angel spoke to Hagar again, telling her not to fear, that God would still fulfill His promise to make Ishmael a great nation. Genesis records, "Then God opened her eyes, and she saw a well of water. And she went and filled the skin with water and gave the boy a drink" (Genesis 21:19).

Again, God saw Hagar when she felt unseen. He fulfilled his promise to make Ishmael's life mean something by making him into a great nation. This is significant because Ishmael was not the child of the covenant God made with Abraham and Sarah; yet, God blessed him with a purpose and legacy. Ishmael's life mattered; therefore, Hagar's motherhood mattered.

Hagar's motherhood went unseen by Sarah. Her identity as a mother was in crisis. While she was physically present, she felt invisible. Like many grieving mothers, her motherhood felt unacknowledged. God saw Hagar's pain, her needs, and her motherhood and came close.

After my daughter was born and our family was complete, we often received comments like, "You've got your hands full." I never knew how to answer the question, "Is this your first?" after Samuel was born. Or "Are you going to have more?" after Emma Joy arrived. While these comments and questions weren't intended to sting, they often did. Only one side of my motherhood was being seen and acknowledged. The two children I was mothering in my heart felt forgotten.

God shows me that the unseen part of my motherhood has not been forgotten every time someone says their names. My unseen motherhood is seen when I receive flowers on a death anniversary or a Facebook comment that remembers what was lost. God reminds me I am seen when one of my living children mentions their brother and sister in heaven. My motherhood feels whole. This feeling of wholeness doesn't mean the pain is gone; it means my story is fully seen.

It's easy to feel forgotten in your unseen motherhood. Where in your motherhood have you felt seen? Where have you felt unseen? Know that you are not forgotten. God sees both the seen and unseen parts of your motherhood.

The Abundant Path: Honoring Both Seen and Unseen Motherhood

There is a layer of grief that comes when the unseen parts of our motherhood are not acknowledged. Our motherhood can feel full, yet incomplete. When those unseen parts of our motherhood are seen and acknowledged, we can experience healing.

You are not alone in navigating this tension between the seen and the unseen parts of motherhood after loss. The practices that follow are not meant to serve as a fix for your fragmented motherhood. They are gentle invitations to help you live with wholeness amid the fragmentation.

Acknowledge the Unseen

As loss moms, it is important to validate the internal work of grieving and mothering our babies who have died. In your journal, name the unseen parts of your motherhood. Make a list identifying moments you have felt invisible. Record how you felt in these moments.

Say Their Name(s)

The lives of babies who died during pregnancy matter and deserve to be recognized. If you have named your baby, say their name(s). This could be in prayer, in your journal, or to your living children. Say their name(s) on anniversaries, holidays, or in ordinary moments when their absence feels heavy. If you haven't named your baby, that's okay too. You can still speak of them using words that feel right to you: "baby," "my little one," or even just "you."

You are allowed to speak your baby's name, even when no one else does. By saying their names, we are making the invisible visible and acknowledging their presence and how they shape our lives and motherhood.

Invite Your Living Children Into the Story

Speaking to your living children about your loss/losses can help normalize grief and remembrance, as well as encourage a connection between heaven and earth.

- Talk about your baby in heaven using age-appropriate language.

- Create shared traditions for honoring and remembering your baby/babies in heaven with your living children. This could include lighting a candle on anniversaries, planting a tree or flower in memory of your little one, drawing a picture, or writing a letter to your baby/babies in heaven.

- Read books about loss and heaven. See the back of the book for a suggested reading list.

Bringing your living children into this part of your story isn't forcing grief. It's modeling wholeness. It allows you to show them that sorrow and joy can exist together.

Remember That You are Seen

Spend some time reading and reflecting on Genesis 16:13. What does it mean to you to be seen by El Roi, the God Who Sees? Record the parts of your motherhood that no one else sees in your journal. What do you long for God (or others) to see and honor in your story?

Write or print out the words "El Roi" and display them somewhere you will see them regularly, like your bathroom mirror, inside your Bible, or taped on the inside cover of your journal. Let this serve as a reminder that your grief, your love, and your motherhood (both the seen and unseen parts) are seen and held by God.

Tell Someone Your Whole Story

Sharing our stories with others can help reduce feelings of isolation and give a voice to the parts of our motherhood that feel invisible. You don't have to share publicly. Find one safe person with whom to share your whole story. Write a letter, have a conversation, or share a journal entry with this person. What do you wish someone knew about your entire story? What unseen parts of your motherhood would you like someone else to see? Sharing your story can be healing and honoring to the life and love you have for your baby.

Pray a Blessing Over Your Motherhood

Set aside a quiet moment to pray a blessing over your motherhood, both the seen and unseen parts. You may choose to write your prayer of blessing in your journal, speak it out loud in a private space, or whisper it in your heart. Use this time to acknowledge your longing, your loss, your love, and your legacy. Praying a blessing over your motherhood can help affirm your identity before God and bring peace to a motherhood that holds joy and sorrow.

Here are some prayer prompts to get you started:

- "Lord, bless this motherhood You have entrusted to me. As I carry children in my arms and in my heart, teach me to hold them all with grace."

- "Thank You, God, for seeing my whole story. Help me honor each of my children and rest in the truth that my motherhood is not broken."

- "Jesus, You know the parts of my motherhood the world does not see. Let my motherhood be a reflection of Your faithfulness."

Parenting after loss means carrying both the seen and unseen parts of motherhood. Being a mother to the children you hold in your arms and the children you hold in your heart is a sacred calling. Sometimes you may feel invisible, fragmented, and unsure of how to honor all of your children. You are not alone in this tension. Your motherhood matters, even the parts no one else sees. Remember the God who sees when your motherhood feels unseen by the world.

CHAPTER 7

Living the Both/And Life

"When the cares of my heart are many, your consolations cheer my soul." – Psalm 94:19

A few days before Thomas Roy should have turned ten, I was at the park with Samuel and Emma Joy. My attention was drawn to a grandmother and her grandchild. The grandmother looked over at the disappointed toddler who didn't want to leave the park and said,

"It's okay. You can feel sad."

As they walked by me, it felt as if that snippet of their conversation was meant for me to hear.

"It's okay. You can feel sad ... even ten years later."

The gravity leading up to the day he should have been turning ten had been present for several weeks. The grief had started showing up in my body as it usually does leading up to significant days in my grief journey. My sleep was disrupted. I felt anxious. My patience was thin.

In the days leading up to November 19, I held onto that grandmother's words, and they served as a permission slip to feel all the feelings the day would bring.

It's okay.

You can still grieve.

You can still ask why.

You can let the tears fall.

You can exit a room when things feel too heavy, even if it is the church sanctuary.

You can still long for what could have been, what should have been.

It's okay.

You can laugh when your son does something goofy.

You can smile when you hear your daughter singing at the top of her lungs in the shower.

You can beam with pride when your children master new things.

You can enjoy making memories with your family, even though your family is incomplete.

It's okay.

You can smile because you're happy.

You can say all the words or say nothing at all.

You can love the life you have and embrace it all—the good and the bad.

It's okay.

Over the years, I have come to see the space where joy and sorrow meet as sacred. I find myself in this space often. There is an ever-present mix of gratitude for how the life and death of two babies I never met changed me, and a regret that I never got to know them. These losses feel like a curse and a gift. It's never either/or. It's always and.

It's okay to wrestle with the tension that arises when joy and sorrow meet. What if this coexistence isn't something to avoid? Perhaps it is something to embrace as you walk forward through grief and strive to live abundantly after loss.

Naming the Tension

Our culture puts a lot of pressure on moving on when bad things happen. When grief enters the story, condolences are expressed, meals are sent, funerals are held, and weeks later, most have forgotten. There is a silent expectation that life must be either/or instead of both/and when it comes to grief. You're either grieving or you're joyful. You're happy or sad, up or down, grateful or longing for something different.

There is a common language used surrounding grief that reinforces this mindset. Some examples are:

"At least you know you can get pregnant."

"It was probably for the best."

"You just need to focus on the good."

"Time heals all wounds."

"God won't give you more than you can handle."

While those saying these things mean well, statements like this are harmful, even if that harm is unintentional. Hearing these things can make grieving mothers feel that they should choose between their pain and their blessings.

These phrases ignore the ongoing presence of grief and leave space for only one emotion at a time. They imply that grieving makes one ungrateful and assume joy must replace sorrow. But that's not the case.

Loss, especially pregnancy loss, doesn't fit into a tidy little box. It's not a one-time thing that happens and we move on from it. The grief from pregnancy loss stays with us. The good news is, we can let conflicting emotions exist without canceling each other out. No matter what the culture tries to convince us of, it is human to feel multiple things at once. We can live in the both/and.

The tension of joy and sorrow shows up in everyday motherhood, anniversaries, holidays, and even unexpected moments. As time goes on, the tension remains.

I have felt this tension while holding my newborn son, watching my children laugh hysterically over something silly, and packing clothes away that my children had outgrown. It's present on birthdays and holidays when the air is filled with excitement, and my heart holds empty spaces for the two babies I never held.

The tension also shows up in unexpected moments. I have cried in church during worship while praising God for His goodness and feeling deep sorrow over my losses. I have beamed with pride watching my daughter perform on stage and my son make a great archery shot as I wondered what hobbies my babies in heaven may have enjoyed.

You don't have to conform to the cultural expectation of either/or after experiencing pregnancy loss. Naming the tension of experiencing multiple emotions at once is an essential step in learning to live fully in the both/and.

Living Fully in the In-Between

To live fully in the both/and, we must first understand what an abundant life after pregnancy loss looks like. An abundant life after loss doesn't mean life is always cheerful, easy, or free of pain. Our culture would have us believe that living fully equals wealth, possessions, success, and happiness. That's exactly how I defined it before grief entered my story.

Now, I've come to see abundant living as a life with purpose, no matter the circumstances. This purposeful life is anchored in believing that God is good through it all. Living abundantly after loss is:

- Being honest and intentional, not in denial.
- Showing up, even when life hurts.
- Accepting the good things that happen and not feeling like letting go of what was lost is necessary.
- Realizing joy does not cancel out sorrow.

You might think abundance means sadness doesn't exist. Or if you're still grieving, your faith isn't strong enough. Maybe you feel that if you love the life you have now, you will forget everything you lost. Grief tries to tell us these lies and limit our ability to live fully.

We can begin to embrace an abundant life after loss when we make room for joy and sorrow to coexist. So what does this look like in real life?

On a recent vacation to Florida, I encountered joy and sorrow as I watched my children enjoy playing in the waves and the sand. Their excitement was contagious. As I observed them having the time of their lives, I felt a twinge of sadness as I thought about the two who were missing and wondered what a beach trip with four children would be like.

Unlike in my early years of life after loss, these moments rarely take me by surprise anymore. I've come to expect them. I felt peace as I breathed in the salty air and made space for joy and sorrow. I could enjoy the moment and wonder about what could have been at the same time without feeling guilty for feeling one way or the other.

Trying to feel one way or another and believing life has to be either/or can be suffocating. Accepting both/and while creating a space where joy and sorrow can coexist feels like a giant exhale.

Where are you holding your breath? Do you hide your sadness because you feel others will think you should be okay? Have you held back joy because you felt you would betray your grief? Are you scared of what might happen if you create space to hold joy and sorrow?

Embracing joy and sorrow requires a leap of faith. When we take that leap, God is with us. Holding joy and sorrow together creates a sacred space where God can meet us and bring us closer to Him. The tension does not mean you are a failure. Living in the tension is a faithful and necessary step for moving forward.

You don't have to get over your loss to find peace. If sorrow still lingers, you are not a failure. If moving forward and embracing joy and sorrow feels scary, you're not alone. Let God meet you here as abundance takes root in your life.

A Biblical Example of Both/And: Naomi

The story of Naomi found in the book of Ruth is an example from Scripture of living the both/and life. When we meet Naomi, we learn that she, her husband, and her two sons traveled from Bethlehem to Moab to escape a famine. Her husband died, and her sons married Moabite women. Ten years later, both of her sons died. She was in a foreign place that was not her home, and she had lost her husband and her sons. Her life had been turned upside down.

Naomi decides to journey back to Bethlehem accompanied by her daughter-in-law, Ruth. Even though she has returned to where she feels most comfortable and at home, she still carries great sorrow. She is in so much pain that she changes her name:

> She said to them, "Do not call me Naomi; call me Mara, for the Almighty has dealt very bitterly with me. I went away full, and the Lord has brought me back empty. Why call me Naomi, when the Lord has testified against me and the Almighty has brought calamity upon me?" (Ruth 1:20-21)

The name "Naomi" means pleasant, and "Mara" means bitter.[16] In this moment, Naomi expresses great sorrow over her loss, and she acknowledges the sovereignty of God for bringing her home. She speaks openly about her pain. Naomi's circumstances at the beginning of the book of Ruth highlight the complexity of feeling both held and abandoned.

In chapter 2, Naomi begins a transformation from despair to hope to renewed joy. Ruth went to glean from Boaz's field. When she returns with grain and food and tells Naomi how kindly Boaz treated her, Naomi begins to find hope again. We see this in verse 20 as she blesses Ruth: "And Naomi said to her daughter-in-law, 'May he be blessed by the Lord, whose kindness has not forsaken the living or the dead!' Naomi also said to her, 'The man is a close relative of ours, one of our redeemers.'" She guides Ruth in interacting with Boaz in hopes of his redeeming Ruth. These actions begin to reflect a change in Naomi that leads to healing, even though she still holds sorrow.

Naomi's transformation isn't sudden; instead, it's a slow shift to living in the both/and. Naomi never says she no longer feels bitterness toward her circumstances; however, we can see the change through her behavior. The highlight of Naomi's redemption story comes with the birth of Boaz and Ruth's child, Obed. The joy and redemption that came with the birth of this child are recognized by the women in Naomi's community in Ruth 4:14-15:

> Then the women said to Naomi, "Blessed be the Lord, who has not left you this day without a redeemer, and may his name be renowned in Israel! He shall be to you a restorer of life and a nourisher of your old age, for your daughter-in-law who loves you, who is more to you than seven sons, has given birth to him."

God was faithful to Naomi amid her grief. He led Ruth to be loyal to Naomi. He provided Ruth with a new husband, securing Naomi's future. Obed's birth was a source of joy and comfort. Naomi's restoration did not erase her sorrow. It allowed her to live in the both/and. Obed did not replace her sons or fill the hole in her heart left by their deaths, but he did play a role in her healing.

We can learn a lot from Naomi's story as we move forward after loss and step into the both/and life. Naomi's story gives us permission to feel deep loss and deep joy at the same time. We see that Naomi did not have to get over losing her husband and sons to experience redemption. Neither do you. Through Naomi's story, we see that restoration is not the absence of pain, but the presence of hope within the pain. Being open to God's restoration and redemption after loss does not mean the pain is gone.

Living the Both/And in Daily Life

Choosing to live fully in the both/and isn't a one-time decision. It's a daily decision to keep moving forward in grief, no matter what life throws at you. Sometimes the tension shows up in big ways, but it often finds you in the small, ordinary moments.

Joy and sorrow intertwine as you thank God for your blessings and also whisper, "I miss them." Sometimes, it's a quiet ache in sacred routines.

It's the moment you glance up at the memorial ornament on the tree as you watch your living children hang their special ornaments.

Other times, the tension shows up unexpectedly and stops you in your tracks. You're at the park watching your living children play, and hear another mom call out the name of your baby in heaven. You are forced to pause as you wonder how life would be with them here.

It can also break its way through the happiest moments. It's the tears that well up when you hear a song on the radio that triggers grief when moments before you were laughing with your children.

And there are other moments you try to hold it all in one place on the page, in your prayers, and in your heart. It shows up in a journal entry that is full of gratitude and also acknowledges the ache of your loss.

These moments, some subtle and some sudden, are not signs of weakness. Their appearance doesn't mean you are stuck in the past. They are opportunities for you to be held by the One who understands. Offer these moments to God and let Him meet you in the tension. These moments invite us into deeper faithfulness, not because the pain is resolved, but because we are willing to feel it.

The Abundant Path: Choosing Both/And

The tension created by the coexistence of joy and sorrow isn't something that needs to be fixed. It's something we learn to live with. These practices are meant to help you live fully in the both/and as you move forward. Remember not to view them as a checklist, instead as suggestions to help you create space to stay present in the both/and moments of daily life as you recognize that God meets you there.

Name the Both/And

Recognizing and naming the moments of tension are vital for learning to live fully in the both/and. Pause once a day and identify two seemingly conflicting emotions you are holding. There's no need to explain them or make them match. You just need to name them. Write down the feelings.

"I feel thankful and exhausted."

"I feel full, but also long for more."

"I feel joyful and full of sadness."

Acknowledging and naming these opposite emotions helps normalize the layered emotions that come after loss. When you name the tension without trying to explain it, you practice emotional honesty without judgment and take a huge step toward moving forward.

Take a Sacred Pause

Choose a time to take a two-minute pause every day. This could be during your morning coffee, after school drop-off, or right before bed. Pray this short prayer:

"God, meet me in the middle of joy and sorrow."

Then sit in the stillness of God's presence.

This practice trains your heart to rest in God's presence instead of striving for resolution. It allows you to cultivate stillness and become aware of God's presence in the tension.

Scripture for the Tension

When you are caught in the tension, pause and return to God's Word. Choose one or more of the scripture passages below to read and reflect upon. Write the passages on a note card, in your journal, or add them to a note in your phone so that you can easily return to them when your emotions feel too big to name.

2 Corinthians 4:8-10

Psalm 126:5-6

Lamentations 3:21-23

Habakkuk 3:17-18

John 16:20, 22

When you root your emotional tension in Scripture, you open yourself up to experiencing God's presence within the tension.

Carry a Daily Anchor

Sometimes something physical can help remind us of the truth we've read. Find a small, tangible object you can keep with you to symbolize the both/and you are holding. This could be a small stone, shell, piece of jewelry, or charm. Touch or look at it when the tension feels especially heavy. Let it remind you that you can hold both conflicting emotions; you don't have to choose one over the other. This helps physically anchor the reality that joy and sorrow can be carried together.

Explore What Else is True

During moments when you find yourself experiencing grief that is too heavy or the pressure to be okay is too strong, pause and ask, "What else is true?" Let this question guide you in seeing the bigger picture. Write down how you are feeling, followed by what else is true. Use this practice when one negative emotion is dominating and you want to open up your awareness to what else is present. This will help extend your emotional lens while still validating your feelings.

Bless the Tension

Write or speak aloud during prayer a simple blessing that honors the joy and sorrow you are carrying. Your words don't have to be perfect, just honest. This serves as a way of naming the truth and inviting God into this space with you.

Here are some prompts to get you started:

"Bless the warmth I felt this morning, and bless the tears I cried this afternoon."

"Bless the ache for what is lost, and bless the gift I hold today."

"Bless the longing to remember, and bless my willingness to move forward."

Speaking a blessing over the tension helps release the pressure to resolve it and offers it a sacred space for God to dwell. Blessing the tension helps honor the fullness of your experience.

Name it With Someone.

Find a friend or family member who will share the tension with you. Each week, share a both/and moment with them. Let them hold it with you. Be sure to let them know you aren't seeking a resolution to the tension. You just need someone to share it with. Being seen in the middle of the tension is part of healing. This practice helps break isolation and reminds us we are not alone in the complexity of the tension. Carrying joy and sorrow becomes something shared instead of something carried in silence.

It's possible to live fully in the tension of joy and sorrow. You can embrace the both/and life without resolving the tension. Just as the grandmother at the park permitted the upset toddler to feel sad, I'm offering you permission to live in the both/and.

It's okay to move forward in the tension. You are not a failure if you feel the tension of conflicting emotions. The goal isn't to get over your loss but to live faithfully through it. This middle space in the tension is sacred. I invite you to embrace it and allow God to meet you here.

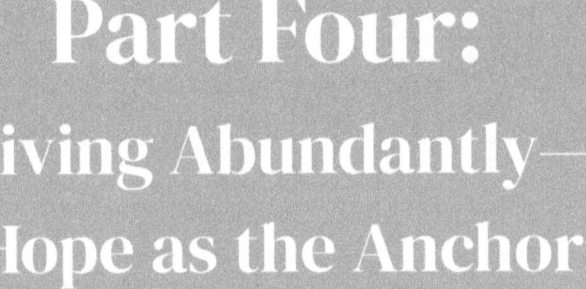

Part Four:

Living Abundantly—
Hope as the Anchor

CHAPTER 8

Sometimes He Takes Us Back

"I will remember the deeds of the Lord; yes, I will remember your wonders of old. I will ponder all your work, and meditate on your mighty deeds." – Psalm 77:11-12

I never expected a hole-in-the-wall BBQ joint hidden off a Florida highway to become an Ebenezer. But that's exactly what Captain's BBQ became on a brisk February day in 2020.

Thirteen months after Thomas Roy died, I found out I was pregnant for the second time. The same week we found out I was pregnant, two weeks before we were to leave for a vacation to Florida, I found out I was miscarrying the baby.

We decided to take the trip despite the sorrow over another failed pregnancy. I tried to make the most out of our vacation as we took the trolley around St. Augustine, tried different restaurants, and laughed at the funny way the GPS said "Ponce de Leon," but the anxiety was high, and sadness loomed despite my best efforts.

Toward the end of our trip, we decided to ride along the A1A and see where it would lead. We ended up at a little hole-in-the-wall bait and tackle shop that doubled as a BBQ restaurant. It was well past lunchtime, so we decided to try it.

A storm came as we waited for our food on the screened-in porch. I felt so empty inside as I sat there watching the rain pour down. Life felt heavy, and my body felt numb. Here we were again, living with the aftermath of the death of another precious baby we never even got to hold. This time, we never got to tell the world about her life before her death. We sat in silence as I held back tears.

Why did this happen?

How long will it take to get pregnant next time?

Will I ever be able to carry a pregnancy to term?

Will I ever get to be a mother to living children?

Will I survive this?

Will we survive this?

Fast forward six and a half years ...

Our minivan pulled into the sandy parking lot, and I hopped out and took a picture of the sign. I had a feeling I was going to want to remember this moment. We didn't expect to return here. A quick Google search showed we were nearby, and the place was still open, so we figured, "Why not?"

We placed our order and waited on the same screened-in porch where we had sat years before; only now, there were four of us. It wasn't raining this time. The sun reflected brightly off the water as a gentle breeze blew through the mossy trees. I snapped a picture of my family looking out at the water.

I watched as these beautiful children, whom I prayed so many prayers for, took in the scene. As I watched them, I realized this was a picture of redemption. It was a scene I could not have imagined all those years ago. Tears welled up in my eyes, and my heart nearly exploded because it was the most beautiful scene in the most beautiful redemption story.

Our food arrived, and we ate our lunch. Then we walked out toward the water. I watched in awe as my four-year-old daughter and five-year-old son played on a playground nearby. We walked around the property for a while before returning to the van and heading home.

Who knew a little BBQ place on the side of the highway in the middle of nowhere could elicit such emotion? Returning to this place was like taking a victory lap and showing my sad thirty-something self of six and a half years before that we had made it—we survived. Going back there was a reminder that God writes the best stories.

The first time we visited, I had no idea this place would be significant in our story. It was just a stop for lunch amid a tumultuous time in my life.

God brought us back. Our return reminded me of what was lost and showed me what He redeemed. Sometimes, He takes us back to remind us how far we've come. Sometimes, He takes us back to remind us that He is in control. Sometimes, He takes us back to remind us the story isn't over yet. Sometimes, He takes us back.

Living in the Redemption

I think of our return to Captain's BBQ often. Returning there taught me that God places Ebenezers along our journey to teach us to remember. The memory of returning to that place while living the life I dreamed of living shows God's redemption. When this memory comes to mind, my heart is comforted knowing God is in the details. He is in control of every aspect of our story.

Reflecting on God's redemption reminds me that I am a different mother because I have two babies in heaven. Losing them not only transformed me as a person but also changed how I approach motherhood. Every day with my living children is a gift. Recognizing their lives and our time together as a gift doesn't mean we are exempt from hard moments or that everything is plcasant. It means we embrace it all as it comes—the good and the bad.

When my daughter was a toddler, bedtime often became drawn out as she requested song after song as I tucked her into bed. My heart felt full when I looked down at her, dressed in onesie pajamas and gripping her precious stuffed bunny, Bun-Bun. It also felt a little empty as I thought about the two babies I never got to tuck into bed. I didn't mind the prolonged bedtime routine because it served as another reminder that joy and sorrow can co-exist and that God is faithful.

This perspective shaped my mindset, as well as how I showed up in motherhood, especially on the hard days. In the moments when mothering is difficult, I can step back and remind myself that this is the life I prayed for. I can take a deep breath in the middle of a tantrum and know that this too shall pass. When worry over my children threatens to take over my thoughts, I can remember that God is in control.

Mothering after loss has played a role in shaping my children's faith. I have been able to use our experience to pass on my eternal perspective to my children. We have talked about their siblings in heaven their entire lives. They know that death is a part of life, but it's not the end. We often talk about the fact that this world is not our forever home—heaven is. We talk about the day our family will be complete when we all get to heaven.

Living life with an eternal perspective has not erased the pain of losing my babies. Moments of joy and sorrow arise often. They show up in the big moments like birthdays and Christmas, and everyday moments like playing outside or enjoying a book together. I have learned to stay rooted in hope while acknowledging the pain. When I wonder how life would be with all four of my children here, I remind myself that I am a different mother than I would have been had they all lived.

Living in redemption means remembering where we have been while completely embracing where we are. When joy and sorrow fill the same moment, when tears of grief and smiles of gratitude show up at the same time, I don't shy away from it. I don't try to rush the moment away. I sit in it and remember the then and the now.

Remembering the then and the now helps anchor me in God's promises. When hard moments come, I can reflect on how far I've come as a child of God and as a mother. God promises to go with me and never leave nor forsake me. Knowing this helps me keep moving forward with hope.

The Role of Remembering in Rebuilding Hope

Remembering the past isn't just a sentimental return to what was. It is not going back and dwelling in the past. Looking back doesn't have to serve as a painful reminder of all we've been through. It can be a sacred way to mark our journey forward. God calls us to remember so we can see how far we have come.

We did not plan to return to that BBQ restaurant that February day, but I'm grateful we did. Nothing happens by coincidence. God knew we would return to that place. He knew this experience of remembering would serve as an affirmation of growth and healing. Returning there brought the pain of our first visit to my mind; however, the pain wasn't overwhelming. It didn't reopen the wounds of losing my first two babies, but it affirmed the growth and healing that had taken place in my life.

Looking back won't be the same for everyone. It could be a moment marked by loss or by healing. It could be a moment that holds both joy and sorrow. Remembering is an invitation to reflect, not to regress. It's an invitation to see our pain from a different perspective. You may be prompted to look back through a song, a smell, or a person. For me, returning to a physical place was part of the healing. For others, remembering could happen during a quiet moment of reflection or a conversation.

Remembering has taught me to look for God's faithfulness in the hard parts of my story. One of the biggest fears I had as I began my grief journey was that I would forget my babies. Initially, remembering was painful. Now I can look back on the past with hope. Painful memories still surface, but I can see how God used the pain to make me better. Remembering the past is a gift that affirms progress made on the road to healing.

A Biblical Example of Returning to Remember: Jacob's Return to Bethel

Jacob's return to Bethel is a biblical example of returning to remember. Jacob first encountered God at Bethel when he was fleeing his brother Esau. He stopped in Haran to rest and used a stone as a pillow.

While sleeping, he dreamed of a ladder leading to heaven. God appeared to Jacob in this dream and promised him land and blessings. When Jacob woke up, he set up the stone as an altar to God, renamed the place Bethel (meaning House of God),[17] and worshiped God there.

Years later, God told Jacob to return to Bethel and make an altar for Him there. Jacob returned to Bethel and built an altar to honor God. Once again, God appeared to Jacob and renamed him Israel, signifying that a nation would come from him.

Returning to Bethel was important to Jacob. He instructed his family, "Then let us arise and go up to Bethel, so that I may make there an altar to the God who answers me in the day of my distress and has been with me wherever I have gone"(Genesis 35:3). Bethel was the place where God made a promise to Jacob in his distress. Returning there allowed Jacob to look back and see that God kept His promise. Jacob set up an altar there to remember God's faithfulness.

Like Jacob, I returned to a place I never expected to see again. It was a place God knew I needed to return. For Jacob, Bethel was the place where God first spoke His promises over him. For me, the screened-in porch of Captain's BBQ was at first a place of deep sorrow. It became a place where I could see that God kept His promises. A place of sorrow was turned into a marker of healing. While I didn't build a physical altar, I experienced a holy moment with God that left me filled with gratitude and in awe of His goodness.

Experiencing a full-circle moment as I did that day was a powerful reminder of my healing journey. This moment became a spiritual marker for me because it helped me see how far I had come. It helped me see that I could reframe a painful memory to see the good. Having these spiritual markers in our lives can help us remember who God is. They can help ground us when our circumstances feel uncertain. When hope feels distant, they can restore our eternal perspective.

While we may not build physical altars today, we can use things to mark the sacred moments we experience. This could be done through journaling, creating art, or praying a specific prayer. Returning to these markers helps us live abundantly. They are not just markers of pain. They are proof of progress. We can use them to reflect on how far we have come.

Our Ebenezers serve to show us God's presence in our stories. These markers of remembrance go beyond personal healing. They equip us to offer hope to others. Looking back can sometimes feel scary, but I have found reflecting on the past to be a powerful tool in moving forward toward the abundant life God has called us to live. Is God inviting you to look back? Maybe it's not to grieve again, but to mark His presence. As you look back, ask God to show you what He wants you to see.

Redemption in the Everyday

Redemption doesn't only show up in the full circle moments like I experienced at Captain's BBQ. It can be found in the everyday. My moment of remembrance prompted me to look for God's redemption on a regular basis. I am often reminded of God's restoration and healing work in my life.

When we look, we can see redemption at work in ordinary moments. My grief journey has caused me to approach nearly every aspect of my life differently, including motherhood. My priority as a mother is to point my children to Jesus. Mothering after loss means

I parent with eternity in mind. Reflecting on God's redemptive work helps me accomplish my goals as a mother.

Even though I live with new priorities and a deeper perspective, grief still lingers. Recognizing God's redemption doesn't erase grief. It helps reframe grief through God's presence. Even on the best days (sometimes especially the best ones), I still ache for what could have been.

When the four of us celebrate Thanksgiving wearing fancy clothes and using the fancy dishes, I still see two empty seats at the table. Redemption reminds me that one day those seats will no longer be empty. I can hold gratitude for what is and longing for what cannot be without feeling guilty for holding both.

When looking for redemption in the everyday, we can identify small areas of growth that once felt impossible. For the longest time, even after my living children were born, it was difficult for me to be around babies. Seeing a baby still reminded me of the babies I longed to hold but never had the chance. I can now smile at a mother with a newborn as I remember holding and nurturing my living children when they were babies. This is progress. This is God's redemptive work in the everyday.

Think about the ways you are different from the way you were in your earliest days of grief. What have you learned to carry and what have you been able to release? For me, sometimes it's something simple, like smiling at a mother and her newborn. This is a small shift that shows healing. Often healing begins with noticing, and redemption appears quietly. Are there areas of your life where God is writing redemption into your daily story—even if they feel small?

The Abundant Path:
Living in Remembrance and Redemption

Living in remembrance and redemption doesn't require big gestures. Remembrance and redemption are ongoing, intentional actions. This often begins with quiet, sacred rhythms. These practices are meant to help you hold space for joy and sorrow, recognizing God's presence in the middle of it all. Choose one or two of these practices to try. This isn't about doing more but noticing more.

Return to a Place that Once Held Only Sorrow

Return somewhere—either physically, emotionally, or spiritually—that once held sorrow. This could be a place or even a moment in your memory. As you return, ask God to help you see this place with new eyes. Ask Him to show you where healing has taken place. Reflect on how you have changed since then. Remember that returning doesn't mean reliving the pain. Remembering can be a way of honoring your progress and acknowledging God's presence in your journey.

Create a Remembrance Ritual

Creating and implementing sacred rhythms can help ground us and help us mark God's faithfulness. These rituals don't have to be elaborate. They serve as an invitation to pause, remember, and receive God's comfort. Here are some ideas for remembrance rituals:

- Light a candle on significant dates like death anniversaries or due date anniversaries.

- Play a special song when you feel yourself drifting toward sorrow. Music can be powerfully healing.

- Take a prayer walk and talk to God about what you miss and what brings you gratitude.

Write a Then-and-Now Reflection

Journaling is a powerful tool in recording your healing journey. Take some time to write down where you were in your early days of grief. What did you fear? What did you long for? What felt impossible? Then, write about where you are now. What has softened? What is still hard? Where have you seen God's redemption? This is your Ebenezer. It serves as a written altar declaring, "God has helped me this far."

Notice Small Shifts Toward Redemption

Redemption often shows up quietly. Start paying attention to moments that once unraveled you but now pass by with a little more peace. It could be a memory that no longer stings as sharply as it once did. Maybe it's a trigger that still brings tears, but not complete despair. It could be a moment that brings a smile instead of sadness. These are small, sacred signs of progress. Write them down to remind you that healing is happening, even if it is slow.

Say Their Name

Saying the names of the ones we have lost is powerful. It keeps them close and honors their place in your life. Don't be afraid to speak their names in conversation, in prayer, or in stories you share with your living children. Saying their name doesn't mean you are stuck in the past. It means you are carrying them forward with you.

Create a Visual Marker of Redemption

Sometimes we need something tangible to serve as a reminder of our redemption. These visual markers can become places to pause, pray, and reflect when sorrow feels overwhelming. They can remind us that God met us here. Some ideas for a visual marker are:

- Plant a flower or tree in your garden.

- Frame a meaningful photo or quote.

- Write a verse or memory on a stone and keep it somewhere special.

- Write memories, prayers, or milestones on slips of paper and keep them in a jar.

- Paint, sketch, or create a digital collage using images representing joy and sorrow.

Share Your Story

Sharing your redemption story can help bring light to someone walking through the darkness. You don't have to have it all figured out. Telling the truth about where you've been and where God met you can be powerful. Healing can happen when we speak hope aloud.

When I look back on my Bethel moment at Captain's BBQ, I am still in awe of the story God is writing in my life. He truly writes the best stories, even when we don't always see it. He is not finished. My story is still being written. Even if you can't see the full picture yet, beauty is unfolding in your story, too. Look for what God is doing in the quiet, unfinished moments. Remember that redemption doesn't erase sorrow. Redemption helps transform our sorrow into a bigger, more beautiful story.

CHAPTER 9

Unshakeable Hope

"We have this hope as an anchor for the soul, firm and secure."
– Hebrews 6:19 (NIV)

The air was crisp, and the jacket I was wearing did not adequately shield the chill of the wind, but I was being pulled to take a walk. This wasn't just an ordinary walk. It was a Sunday morning at church during Sunday School. I often felt this pull when I was lost in grief and my emotions threatened to overtake me. These walks served to clear my head and talk to God. God often used these walks to help me see things from a different perspective.

As I walked down the drive toward the highway, I was led to the church's historic cemetery. I had done this a few times over the past year—walked among the final resting places of the bodies of the dead. Usually, I walked to the grave sites of my grandparents and aunts and uncles who had made their way to heaven. I would recall fond memories of my childhood as I passed the gravestones with familiar names. I never paid much attention to the others buried there. But something was different this time.

My eye caught a heart-shaped tombstone. Then, I noticed one with little concrete angels perched on top. Another one had lambs etched in the stone. As I noticed the dates on the markers, I realized these were all graves of infants or children. Some had the same birth and death dates. Some only had one date. Others had birth and death dates that were only months or a few years apart. So many infants and children gone in the first minutes, hours, days, weeks, and months of their lives.

Each of them had a story I did not know. Each of them had a mother who was left behind. I did not know the circumstances surrounding their deaths. I guarantee that those mothers did not plan to have to bury their babies. No one plans to bury their baby when they see those two pink lines on a pregnancy test.

One family was buried together. The baby died in 1947, and the mother died in 2015. Sixty-eight years. That mother lived sixty-eight years without her child. What was grief like for her after twenty years? Fifty years? Did tears fall every year on her child's death anniversary? Did she feel a twinge of heaviness every holiday that passed with one missing from the table? Did she talk about her child in the years after the loss? Or did she grieve silently?

At the time, I had lived five years without my first child and four without my second. The idea of walking around with a piece of my heart missing for sixty-eight years felt like an impossible task. Sometimes, walking around with a piece of my heart missing for five more minutes felt impossible.

As I stood there thinking about all the babies and children who never got to grow up here on Earth and all the mothers they left behind, I was reminded that we are not alone. Those of us walking this earth with pieces of our hearts missing are not the only ones. Some of us grieve aloud, while others grieve silently, but we are not alone in our sorrow. We are all missing our babies. God drew me to the cemetery and drew my eye to notice these stones to remind me I am not alone, and grief will last a lifetime.

I turned to head back to the church, still thinking about all the mothers missing their babies, when a single word caught my eye. The word HOPE was carved in all capital letters into one of the gravestones. God spoke to me as I stopped and stared at this single word.

From the moment we heard the words, "It's not good," I began chasing hope. Deep down, I knew hope was all I had.

I think after twenty, thirty, or even sixty years of missing my babies, I will be able to say that hope is what got me through. This is not a frail, questionable, or unstable hope. It is the hope described in Hebrews 6:19—firm, secure, confident, unshakable.

I had to seek out this hope and grab hold of it. I prayed for it. I studied Scripture to understand it. It did not come easily, and now that I have it, I am not letting go. It is a gift from God in the form of His Son, Jesus; without it, I have nothing. Hope is how I get through the next minute, hour, day, week, month, and year.

Hope is how I live after loss.

When Hope Feels Fragile

There was a time after my losses when I thought I'd never get pregnant again. We withstood month after month of failed fertility treatments with nothing to show for it but medical bills and negative pregnancy tests. I was grieving my babies and grieving a body that seemed to keep failing me. Each month that passed was marked with disappointment and despair.

This despair reached its peak in April 2014. We had gone through many rounds of IUI (Intrauterine Insemination) and been unsuccessful every time. In a consultation with my reproductive endocrinologist, he recommended we move on to IVF (In Vitro Fertilization). He sent me home with a white two-pocket folder full of information.

I read every word on every page in that folder when I got home from the appointment. Reading through the information left me feeling overwhelmed, scared, and ... hopeless. We were not prepared for this. Not emotionally, and certainly not financially.

I was able to talk my doctor into holding off on IVF and trying one more round of IUI. We decided to take a break from medical intervention during the month of May and try another IUI in June. While I still held onto a small splinter of hope, I was weary—emotionally, physically, and spiritually.

I know now that my hope back then was circumstantial. I was hoping for something to happen to me. While there's nothing wrong with hoping for good things to happen to us, this kind of hope is not sustainable. It's not unshakeable hope. As soon as the thing we're hoping for doesn't happen or goes away, so does our hope.

Just as I had nowhere to turn but Jesus after Thomas Roy died, I had nowhere else to put my hope as I felt my dream of mothering living children slipping away with every negative pregnancy test. I was forced to imagine a world where I only mothered dead babies. I had to face some tough questions.

How could a life without children here on Earth still be fulfilling?

Could Keith and I make it just the two of us and the deep pain of our losses?

Was Jesus enough if every dream I had for my life was stripped away?

These questions attempted to pull me down and hold me back as I tried to keep moving forward. Being forced to think about the life I dreamed of not becoming a reality was almost unbearable. Then something happened that pointed me back to Jesus again.

Shortly after that appointment, my sister gave me a handmade throw knitted by ladies in the prayer shawl ministry of our church. This ministry was made up of women from the church who gathered to knit prayer shawls to be given away to those experiencing hardships (like a cancer diagnosis) as well as life's joys (like the birth of a child). As they knitted each blanket, they prayed for its recipient.

Holding that throw and reading the card that came with it filled me with a sense of peace. Just when I thought my hope was fading, I realized the many prayers of others were holding it together.

Anchoring Yourself in Hope

While my faith grew significantly after losing Thomas Roy and Margaret Rebecca, my struggle to get pregnant threatened my hope in God's plan. I grew more and more weary after every failed attempt at pregnancy. My view of hope had to change. I could no longer put my hope into something happening (a successful pregnancy). I needed a hope greater than my circumstances.

Changing my view of hope was a lot like surrendering control and fully trusting God. It felt like giving up on my dream. I really didn't want a different kind of hope. I wanted the kind of hope I had to be enough. But God wasn't asking me to stop hoping. He was asking me to change where that hope was anchored.

The hope I needed wasn't a feeling or a mood. I needed hope to be a foundation on which to build a life of faith. I needed to anchor my hope in the One who was holding it all together. This kind of anchored hope takes work.

I began to take small steps toward anchoring my hope in Christ. This started by opening up to others even more about my struggles. I had shared our journey fairly openly up until this point, but I never really shared in real time. I always shared after the fact. Knowing people at church were praying for me, I began requesting prayer beyond my inner circle. I shared openly on social media my struggles and frustrations in becoming pregnant and began asking for prayer when a medical intervention was taking place.

Letting others into the struggle did not feel like an act of desperation. It felt like an act of faith. As I was being held up by the prayers of others, I slowly began to believe in the hope spoken of in Romans 8. The hope Paul talks about is a hope we can hold onto in the middle of our suffering. It's an expectation that God will keep His promises. It's a belief that the glory to come is better than anything we can imagine.

I had not let go of my dream to become pregnant again and mother living children. I loosened the grip I had on my desires and began placing them into the hands of Jesus. In doing that, my hope shifted to an eternal hope in Him. I internalized Romans 8:18, "For I consider that the sufferings of this present time are not worth comparing with the glory that is to be revealed to us." I began to truly believe that the life everlasting waiting for me in heaven far outweighs any of my earthly desires.

Bringing fellow believers into the struggle and rooting myself in prayer and Scripture were key in shifting my focus from "God, make this happen" to "God, hold me through this." My circumstances didn't change right away, but my heart posture did change. As my heart softened and I began to let God hold me through the pain, I began to believe I would be okay regardless of how my story unfolded.

This heart change did not happen overnight or after one prayer or one revelation after studying Scripture. Anchoring our hope in Jesus is an ongoing process. It's normal for our hope to become untethered. As imperfect humans, it's easy to get caught up in the happenings of this life and lose sight of what is waiting for us in the next. We get frustrated when things don't go our way. When my hope begins to feel like it's becoming untethered, I return to prayer and Scripture to redirect my hope to the eternal instead of circumstantial.

A Biblical Example of Anchored Hope: Simeon and Anna

We can look at the lives of Simeon and Anna for a biblical perspective on anchored hope. We find their story in Luke 2 when Mary and Joseph brought Jesus to the temple in Jerusalem to present Him to the Lord and offer a sacrifice according to the Law regarding firstborn males laid out in Exodus 13. Simeon and Anna, both devout believers who had waited their entire lives for the Messiah, were in the temple that day.

Luke tells us that Simeon was righteous, devout, and filled with the Holy Spirit. He was eagerly awaiting the Messiah's arrival, which would bring Israel's rescue. The Holy Spirit had revealed to him that he would see the Messiah before he died. Luke says the Holy Spirit led Simeon to the temple at the same time Mary and Joseph were there with Jesus. Simeon knew Jesus was the Messiah and praised God for fulfilling the promise made by the Holy Spirit.

We aren't told how much time passed between the promise made that Simeon would see the Messiah and its fulfillment. We only know that he faithfully waited to meet the Messiah. Day after day, Simeon lived his life with the hope of rescue. It was a hope anchored in God's promises, not Simeon's circumstances.

Simeon's obedience to the Holy Spirit's prompting led him to the temple, where he met Jesus. He knew Jesus was the Messiah, and he praised God for fulfilling His promise:

Lord, now you are letting your servant depart in peace,

according to your word;

for my eyes have seen your salvation

that you have prepared in the presence of all peoples,

a light for revelation to the Gentiles,

and for glory to your people Israel. (Luke 2:29-32)

Anna, a prophetess, was also in the temple that day. We learn from Luke 2 that Anna was older and had become a widow after only being married for seven years. She had no husband and no children. I imagine her life did not turn out the way she planned or dreamed. Yet, she spent day and night at the temple worshiping, praying, and fasting. Her hope was anchored in God, and this showed through her actions. This hope was a lifestyle, not just a longing.

Just like Simeon, Anna's faithfulness was rewarded when she saw the promised Messiah. Upon seeing Jesus, she excitedly expressed thanksgiving to God: "And coming up at that very hour she began to give thanks to God and to speak of him to all who were waiting for the redemption of Jerusalem" (Luke 2:38).

What can we learn from Simeon and Anna's responses to seeing their hope fulfilled? Simeon's response is one of release. His life can end peacefully because God's promise was made good. We don't know if Simeon received everything he longed for in life. We do know that God was faithful to Simeon, and, based on his response, God's faithfulness was enough.

Through Anna's life, we see that while she waited quietly for God to fulfill His promise, she could not keep it to herself once the promise was fulfilled. Her anchored hope became her witness. Her worshipful waiting became part of her testimony.

Both Simeon and Anna model a hope that doesn't demand circumstances to be changed, but believes that promises will be fulfilled. We also see that hope is not passive. Hope worships and obeys while it waits and watches.

Choosing Hope Daily

Hope isn't something that comes easily for me every single day, but it is something I return to daily. It's easy for me to begin to feel untethered, especially when the sting of grief shows up. When grief gets heavy, it has a way of making me feel like I can't go on. It threatens to make me lose all hope as I get stuck in my circumstances and not in God's promises.

On days like this, I find myself back in the cemetery, wondering how I can keep moving forward with pain so deep. How will I survive one more day, week, or year without my babies? I ask myself why it still hurts so badly so many years later. I grow tired and weary as I try to hold on to hope.

When I feel my hope slipping away, I have to reach out and reclaim it. I do that by reminding myself of these truths:

- This pain is temporary.
- This world is not my home.
- My babies are safe in the arms of Jesus.
- Every day, I am one day closer to heaven.

Sometimes I write them down. Other times, I speak them aloud. Every time I bring these truths to the surface, my hope is strengthened.

Whether you're newly grieving or you've been grieving for years, you are not behind. And you are not alone. Maybe at this point in your journey, you feel like you've lost all hope. Maybe you don't feel strong enough to choose hope.

When have you felt anchored, even in the smallest moment?

What helps you feel God's presence when grief is overwhelming?

Are there any truths you can hold onto that will help you choose hope?

Choosing hope doesn't require you to deny your pain. Choosing hope means you are trusting the One who is holding you through the pain.

The Abundant Path: Choosing Hope

Remember that anchored hope doesn't erase your grief. It helps you keep moving forward with grief. These practices are meant to help you return to a hope in the One who holds all things together, even when it feels fragile or far away. Grabbing on to this hope doesn't require strength on your part. It only requires obedience.

Speak a Grounding Truth

Choose one truth you want to come back to when hope fades. Here are some ideas:

"This pain is temporary."

"Heaven is real."

"God's promises are true."

This will help anchor your hope in God's truth rather than your feelings or circumstances. Write it down and speak it aloud when you feel hope slipping away.

Create a Hope List to Record God's Faithfulness

Write down small moments when God has met you in your pain. This could be through Scripture, a prayer, or a kind word. Let this become your hope list that you can refer to when you need to be reminded that He is still holding you. This helps you stay rooted in the habit of remembering what God has already done for you.

Write a Breath Prayer

Create a short, simple prayer rooted in hope. Write it down and pray it when grief or hopelessness arises. This is a quick way to help anchor your hope. Here are some examples:

"God, anchor me in your hope."

"I trust You even though I can't see Your plan."

"My hope is in You, not my circumstances."

Find Hope in Scripture

Choose a verse about hope. Write it down and place it somewhere you will see often. Memorize it for moments when you are overwhelmed. Here are some options:

> Isaiah 40:31
>
> Jeremiah 29:11
>
> Micah 7:7
>
> Romans 5:3-4
>
> Romans 15:13

Ask for Prayer When You Need Anchoring

You don't have to choose hope alone. Galatians 6:2 tells us to "Bear one another's burdens." When you feel like you're losing hope, reach out to a trusted friend and ask for prayer. Let them speak truth over you when you can't find the words. Allowing others to hold you up in prayer can help you feel less alone in your pain.

Speak Your Baby's Name in Prayer

Saying your baby's name in prayer is a gentle way to recognize the ongoing love you have for your baby while anchoring your hope in God's eternal promise. Let this remind you that your motherhood is real, your sorrow is recognized, and your story isn't over.

If your hope feels fragile right now, I want you to know anchored hope is possible even on the hardest days. During my walk through the cemetery in 2017, God showed me that my grief would last a lifetime and hope would get me through.

Hope has guided me through:

- Surrendering control and trusting God,
- Walking in anchored faith,
- Letting my grief speak,
- Reframing grief,
- Honoring my grief in body and spirit,
- Honoring my seen and unseen motherhood,
- Choosing both/and,
- Living in remembrance and redemption, and
- Choosing hope.

It is hope that makes it all possible. Holding onto hope in the One who loves me beyond anything I can comprehend, has good plans for me, and keeps His promises is how I have learned to live abundantly after pregnancy loss.

Carrying a baby in your heart and not your arms is excruciating, but it doesn't have to be hopeless. Hope is here for you to take hold of and live the abundant life Jesus's death and resurrection made possible. All you have to do is reach for Him. He's waiting with open arms.

Still in Pieces,
Still Being Mended

"He heals the brokenhearted and binds up their wounds."
– Psalm 147:3

As I was in the middle of writing this book, I attended a retreat that focused on Sabbath rest. We spent the weekend at a beautiful lake house on Lake Keowee in the upstate of South Carolina. We spent a lot of time in silence, attuned to what God wanted us to hear aside from the words of others. It was a beautiful time of community with fellow believers.

One day, we did an art project modeled after the Japanese practice of kintsugi. Kintsugi means "join with gold."[18] This art form takes broken pieces of pottery or glass and pieces them together using gold lacquer, ultimately creating something beautiful from something broken.

For our project, we used inexpensive plates that the instructor broke beforehand. After piecing our plates back together, we joined them with superglue. Then we painted over the cracks with resin mixed with gold-colored mica powder.

As we progressed through the project, I found many parallels to my life after loss.

Putting the broken pieces back together wasn't easy. At times, it was hard to see how they would all fit together again. Throughout my grief journey, there have been times when it has been hard to see how God was working everything together for my good and His glory.

I needed help holding the broken pieces of the plate together while waiting for the superglue to stick. Throughout my grief journey, I have had to rely on others to help me hold it all together.

When I flipped my plate over to paint over the cracks on the back side, it completely fell apart in my hands. I thought the bond was strong and the plate would stay together when I flipped it, but it did not. Throughout my grief journey, there have been times when I thought I had it all together. I thought I was mended until everything fell apart again.

In the end, I used more glue and resin to keep the plate together, but evidence of the broken dish remained. Throughout my grief journey, time has strengthened the mending of my heart, but the proof of my brokenness remains.

I started with a broken plate in many different pieces and ended up with a beautiful piece of art. Just like the Kintsugi art project, my life after loss is a piece of beauty.

I'm still being mended and pieced back together with each passing day. Looking back on my grief journey, I see beauty in the brokenness. I also know the mending isn't finished.

I'm still seeking hope and still finding joy.

An Invitation:
Do You Know My Jesus?

If you've made it this far in my story, you know I have walked through valleys I never imagined or wanted. You've seen how my faith has been tested and how I've learned to live fully in the space where joy and sorrow collide. But you also need to know there is only one reason I've been able to keep moving forward: Jesus.

The hope I have isn't wishful thinking. It's not a "maybe things will get better someday" kind of hope. The hope I carry with me is the steady, anchored, unshakable hope that comes from knowing the One who created me, loves me, and rescued me from my sin.

If you don't know my Jesus yet, I invite you to meet Him today. He will meet you exactly where you are, in the mess, the pain, the confusion, the searching. You don't have to clean yourself up first or have it all figured out. You don't have to wait until the grief subsides or the questions are answered.

The Bible lays out the truth about our need for Him and the path He has forged for us to be forgiven and have eternal life.

1. **We are all sinners.**

   "For all have sinned and fall short of the glory of God." – Romans 3:23

   No one is perfect. We have all missed the mark of God's standard. This sin separates us from God.

2. **Sin comes at a cost.**

   "For the wages of sin is death, but the free gift of God is eternal life in Christ Jesus our Lord." – Romans 6:23

   The debt for our sin is eternal separation from God. But God offers us eternal life through Jesus, a gift we could never earn.

3. **Jesus died for us.**

   "But God shows his love for us in that while we were still sinners, Christ died for us." – Romans 5:8

   God didn't wait for us to have everything together. He loves us so much that He sent Jesus to die in our place and pay the price for our sin.

4. **Salvation is a gift received by faith.**

   "If you confess with your mouth that Jesus is Lord and believe in your heart that God raised him from the dead, you will be saved." – Romans 10:9

   We receive salvation by confessing that Jesus is Lord and believing He rose from the dead. We don't earn salvation by being good enough.

5. **Salvation is for everyone.**

   "For 'everyone who calls on the name of the Lord will be saved.'" – Romans 10:13

It doesn't matter who you are, what your past looks like, or how far you feel from God. The invitation of salvation is for you.

If you're ready to enter into a relationship with Jesus, you can talk to Him right now. Prayer is simply speaking to God from your heart. There's no magic formula or perfect way to pray. All that matters is your sincerity and faith. You might pray something like this:

> *Jesus, I know I am a sinner. I need You. I believe You died for my sins and rose from the dead. I confess that You are Lord of my life. Please forgive me, change me, and help me follow You. I give You my heart, my life, and my future. Thank You for loving me and saving me. Amen.*

If you prayed that prayer and meant it, you now belong to Him. Your circumstances won't change instantly, but your eternity has. You are His. Nothing can separate you from His love (Romans 8:38-39).

If you made this decision today, I would love to celebrate with you and encourage you as you begin this new journey. Please reach out to me. There's a contact page on my website (www.hopehdover.com), and my email is listed there. You don't have to walk this road alone.

This is the greatest hope I know: Jesus loves you, He died for you, and He is with you. He is the only reason I can keep living abundantly after loss, and He will be faithful to you, too.

Sacred Remembering: Say Their Names

Sacred Remembering: Say Their Names

"Behold, I have engraved you on the palms of my hands."
– Isaiah 49:16

R ecently, I sat in a line of vehicles to pick up my kids from a theater day camp they were attending at a local theater ministry. I smiled as one of the teenagers helping with the camp walked by and announced their names over the walkie-talkie. Those were my kids, and I couldn't wait to see how their day at camp went. Unlike my children in heaven, the names of my living children are spoken over and over again each day by me, my husband, each other, and everyone else they encounter.

The names of the babies lost during pregnancy are rarely spoken. These lives mattered. They are not forgotten. The names of these babies deserve to be honored, spoken, and remembered.

I am honored to include the names of these babies we carry in our hearts instead of our arms. These names were submitted by mothers who lost babies through miscarriage, TFMR, stillbirth, and early infancy. These losses span months, years, and even decades. Each name not only represents a life that was lost; it also represents a mother's life that was changed forever.

If your baby's name is not included here, there is space at the end to add it.

Please take a moment to speak each name aloud to remember the life that was lost and the grieving mother who carries that name in her heart.

Thomas Roy Dover May 18, 2012

Margaret Rebecca Dover June 20, 2013

Isaac February 12, 2024

Baby Willis March 2019

Isla Mae August 18, 2019

Junior B September 5, 2020

Baby A February 2016

Baby November 23, 1982

Ian Charles March 1, 2025

James William Garrett June 10, 2013

Gabrielle Garrett October 2017

Baby Girl Garrett June 2020

Pickle October 14, 2023

Caitlin Faith Carter July 17, 2008

Poppy June 2024

Baby Carter November 19, 2020

Baby Childers July 1983

Baby Childers November 1983

Baby Childers October 1990

Calvin Archer Spolar May 19, 2010

Erin Leigh December 6, 1974

Luna Rae Sanchez July 23, 2019

Molly James December 2014

Hinley Grace Estes September 1, 2024

Amado December 10, 2020

Baby Wildman April 2024

Lauran Ashton Burns January 18, 1993

Ryleigh Ann Roberts July 15, 2016

Willow Roberts August 20, 2019

Shelby Leigh Roberts March 18, 2020

Baby December 4, 2023

Baby November 9, 2024

Baby "unknown" Allison December 31, 2007

Esme River Furniss April 13, 2024

Isaac Richard Aaron

Amariah Roselie November 7, 2022

Zion February 21, 2024

Charles Richard July 2, 1992

Jacob Christopher Allen April 11th, 2024

Baby Allen November 27th, 2017

Angel Tanner May 12th, 2001

Emory Gael July 21, 2019

Claire Piper Cranford March 15, 2019

Bennie Kenneth Buxton October 26, 2025

Rowan March 25, 2025

Baby Mitchell February 11, 2013

Baby O'Brien October 6, 2017

Regan Anne

Alex

Thomas

Robert Fitzgerald Herlihy January 27, 2006

Merrick June 25, 2016

Catherine Lucille Dover February 5, 2004

Tinsley Louise August 19, 2013

Xavion October 17, 2023

Parker December 12, 2021

Baby July 10, 2024

Nancy Harrell March 10, 2017

Baby Harrell July 18, 2018

Jordan Simpson December 15, 2010

Princeton Simpson November 23, 2012

Savannah Grace Hillery July 29, 2013

Alaya Barnes March 3, 2017

Asher August 13, 2024

Baby Smith March 20, 1991

Baby Gould July 27, 1994

Cade (Arcadia) May 27, 2024

Elijah October 2017

Abagail Scism April 28

Rachel Ann Davis June 4, 1999

Philip Thomas DeLong 1990

Mary Nell DeLong 1996

Sarah Anne DeLong 1997

Kia March 2007

Harper Melanie August 10, 2018

Evelyn Elizabeth Ballard September 9, 2021

Bethany Lynn Ballard August 28, 2022

Maximilian January 14, 2024

Lukas June 14, 1992

John Patrick Rhodes October 27, 2022

Lucia September 18, 2001

Louie DD June 25, 2014

Leo Hollingsworth June 4, 2025

Grace Marie September 9, 2021

Sophia - Mae April 2016

Baby Wiese September 1, 2023

Baby Wiese June 12, 2024

Henry William Thoms November 20, 2013

Paisley Rae Thoms February 12, 2018

Heaven Baby February 22, 2024

Audrey Grace Upson May 8, 2004

Matthew Quincy January 27, 1979

Jasmine Katrice May 14, 1985

Henry March 30, 2016

Jacob Seth Williams October 13, 2011

Angel Baby January 2017

Angel Baby June 2020

Jeremiah Paul

Twin 1 October 15, 2002

Twin 2 October 15, 2002

Jerry Lewis Smith Jr. December 5, 2003

Baby Brunson March 17, 2014

Graylen Dean Boyd June 4, 2019

Brylin Marie Curnel September 5, 2021

Baby Timmy (Timothy Patrick) November 7, 1992

Lachlan Mcfadyen September 3, 1997

Christina Hamrick February 1997

Olivia Hope Stark November 2004

Baby Stark May 2010

Melissa Diane Miller January 1, 2000

Chloe Grace May 6, 2003

Morgan Faith Plott June 4, 2000

Azariah Charles May 19, 2023

Ryan Jacob Belk November 27, 2008

Nathanial Haberer 2012

Baby 2013

Baby Donahue

Colby Wilhelmus Trecartin December 1, 2019

David Ryan 1993

Samuel Dakota Guy

Chosen Douglas May 17, 2022

Lennox Ichiro Wiggins December 26, 2023

Xavier Cruz Wiggins January 4, 2024

Camden Michael June 30, 2015

Baby Dana July 1981

Baby K

Baby K 2

Joy Vigil April 3, 2014

Alyssa Lynn (girl) or Seth Joseph (boy) April 2006

Rhodes Grubish July 9, 2025

Noah

Caleb

Micah

Baby February 3, 2024

Oliver James Ruppe July 16, 2025

Grace Olivia November 19, 2020

Catherine Isabella June 6, 2021

Jacob June 5, 1999

Joshua Noel December 8, 2022

Unknown January 3, 2024

Baby Greene December 2013

Alivia Agnes July 24, 2008

Zachary Nathaniel February 2, 2010

Heidi Rose December 17, 2005

Baby Brenneman August 27, 2024

Baby Brenneman December 25, 2024

Claire Piper March 11, 2019

Lydia April 21, 2011

Gillian May 5, 2021

Austin April 1997

Emily Grace September 1985

Imogen Dorothy Streiff June 14, 2019

Eva Leigh Schreppel September 20, 2006

Patrick "Rex" Cafardi October 13, 2023

Sammy January 23, 2021

Adrien June 26, 2023

Audrey James Brown March 24, 2023

Eden Jean Brown March 24, 2023

Baby Brown May 20, 2022

Nikki Pettner May 2001

Michael Anthony Pettner November 17, 2002

Hunter

Fisher

Baby Dorr August 28, 2012

Catcher Ryan Mull

Let this space hold the
name(s) you carry in your heart.

Moving Forward: Tools for the Journey

Grief Support Organizations

You do not have to move forward in your grief journey alone. Connecting with others who walk the road of pregnancy loss can play a vital role in healing. I encourage finding an in-person support group. Contact your OB-GYN to see if any support organizations are located near you. I understand in-person support is not readily available everywhere. Below is a list of national organizations that support women and families who have experienced pregnancy loss.

Empty Cradle

Website: emptycradle.org

Empty Cradle offers peer support groups, mentoring, and remembrance events for miscarriage, stillbirth, TFMR, and infant death.

Gathering Hope

Website: gatheringhope.net

Gathering Hope hosts annual gatherings, virtual events, and year-round support for mothers who have experienced pregnancy or infant loss.

Hope After Loss

Website: hopeafterloss.org

Hope After Loss offers support groups, community events, and resources for families experiencing pregnancy and infant loss.

MISS Foundation

Website: missfoundation.org

The MISS Foundation provides support groups, counseling, retreats, and remembrance events for families grieving the death of a child at any age, including pregnancy loss.

Pregnancy After Loss Support (PALS)

Website: pregnancyafterlosssupport.org

PALS offers online communities, peer mentoring, and resources for those pregnant after loss.

Return to Zero: HOPE

Website: rtzhope.org

RTZ Hope offers support groups, retreats, and training for bereaved parents, especially those navigating pregnancy and parenting after loss.

Share Pregnancy & Infant Loss Support

Website: nationalshare.org

Share Pregnancy & Infant Loss Support offers in-person and virtual support groups, memorial events, resources for parents and professionals, and a helpline.

Star Legacy Foundation

Website: starlegacyfoundation.org

Star Legacy Foundations focuses on stillbirth prevention, research, and family support after pregnancy loss and neonatal death. It also offers peer support and professional resources.

Stillbirthday

Website: stillbirthday.com

Stillbirthday Global Network provides a network of trained doulas and chaplains, peer support, and resources for families experiencing any form of pregnancy loss.

Seeking Hope, Finding Joy Playlist

Music has always been healing for me. It can reach places words can't touch. On days when grief feels heavy, a song can remind you you're not alone. In moments when joy sneaks in, it can give you permission to hope again. The right lyrics can hold both joy and sorrow in the same breath, exactly like your heart does every day.

I've gathered these songs from Christian artists to walk with you through the different parts of this journey. The sections match the flow of this book: from the raw ache of loss, to glimpses of redemption, to wrestling with the tension of joy and sorrow, and finally to living abundantly in the hope we have in Christ. My prayer is that as you listen, you'll feel seen, understood, and encouraged to live fully in the sacred space where joy and sorrow collide.

Part One:
The Loss – Experiencing Brokenness

Songs for surrender, lament, and clinging to God in pain

"It Is Well" – Bethel Music

"Blessings" – Laura Story

"I Will Carry You" – Selah

"Even If" – MercyMe

"Held" – Natalie Grant

"Rescue" – Lauren Daigle

"The Hurt & The Healer" – MercyMe

"Come to Jesus" – Chris Rice

"Praise You In This Storm" – Casting Crowns

"Run to the Father" – Cody Carnes

Part Two:
Finding Redemption – Reframing Loss and Hope

Songs for renewal, standing on God's promises, and finding beauty from ashes

"Graves Into Gardens" – Elevation Worship

"See A Victory" – Elevation Worship

"Never Once" – Matt Redman

"Another In The Fire" – Hillsong UNITED

"Find You Here" – Ellie Holcomb

"Raise A Hallelujah" – Bethel Music

"Come What May" – We Are Messengers

"Before the Morning" – Josh Wilson

"Awake My Soul and Sing" – Hillsong Worship

"Great Are You Lord" – All Sons & Daughters

Part Three:
Wrestling with Tension – The Collision of Joy and Sorrow

Songs for both/and living, trusting God, and healing in progress

"Trust In God" – Elevation Worship

"Goodness of God" – Bethel Music & Jenn Johnson

"Make Room" – The Church Will Sing

"There Will Be Joy" – Tauren Wells

"Do It Again" – Elevation Worship

"You're Still God" – Phillips, Craig & Dean

"Sparrows" – Cory Asbury

"Yes I Will" – Vertical Worship

"I Speak Jesus" – Charity Gayle / Here Be Lions

"Whom Shall I Fear" – Chris Tomlin

Part Four:
Living Abundantly – Hope as the Anchor

Songs for unshakeable hope, anchored faith, and joy in Christ

"Hope Has A Name" – River Valley Worship

"Give Me Faith" – Elevation Worship

"God Is Good" – Francesca Battistelli

"The Blessing" – Kari Jobe & Cody Carnes

"Firm Foundation (He Won't)" – Cody Carnes

"Living Hope" – Phil Wickham

"My Hope Is In You" – Aaron Shust

"Standing" – William McDowell

"My Jesus" – Anne Wilson

"Worthy of Your Name" – Passion

Hope Made Possible:
Companions on the Journey

Writing a book that recounts the hardest days of my life was no small feat. I owe much gratitude to the amazing support system God has given me.

To Keith: There aren't adequate words to express my gratitude for your love and support. What could have destroyed us made us stronger in the long run. I love this life we have built together.

To Samuel and Emma Joy: I thank God for the two of you. I am so proud to be your Mommy.

To Mama and Daddy: Your prayers have carried me through every moment of my life—the good, the bad, the easy, the difficult, the joy, and the sorrow. Thank you for the example of a God-honoring life you have given us.

To Sarah and Jane: Thank you for being the best big sisters (and second mamas) a girl could have. You taught me how to be a daughter, sister, wife, mama, and, most importantly, a child of God.

Kenny and Boots: Thank you for the foundation you laid that helped shape Keith into the man he is today. I am grateful for all the support you give us.

Family and Friends: So many held us up in prayer during our most difficult times and celebrated with us during our most joyful times. We will never forget the love and support we have received through the years.

To Brian Dixon: Thank you for following God's call to lead authors into their calling. The ripple effects of your obedience are sure to be immeasurable.

To The hope*books Team: You all are amazing. I am grateful to work alongside you in the good work we are doing. I am thankful for your support and encouragement on this journey.

References

1   Klint, Megan. "God's Sovereignty in Barrenness." *The Center for Bioethics &* *Human Dignity*, 23 May 2024, www.cbhd.org/intersections/gods-sovereign-ty-in-barrenness. Accessed 12 Apr. 2025.

2   *ESV Study Bible: English Standard Version*. Wheaton, IL, Crossway, 2008, 491.

3   "WPC Worships." *YouTube*, uploaded by Westminster Presbyterian Charleston, 22 Mar. 2020, www.youtube.com/watch?v=X8XAIrnOW0g.

4   Apello, Lisa. *Life Can Be Good Again: Putting Your World Back Together After It All Falls Apart*. Minneapolis, Bethany House, 2022, 54.

5   Vroegop, Mark. *Dark Clouds, Deep Mercy: Discovering the Grace of Lament*. Wheaton, IL, Crossway, 2019, 26.

6   Sadock, Elizabeth. "The Cost of Fighting Your Unwanted Emotions." *Psychology Today*, 19 Dec. 2024, www.psychologytoday.com/us/blog/your-body-has-something-to-tell-you/202412/the-cost-of-fighting-your-unwant-ed-emotions. Accessed 1 June 2025.

7   Dembling, Sophia. "Grief Is Physical, Too." *Psychology Today*, 13 May 2022, www.psychologytoday.com/us/blog/widows-walk/202205/grief-is-physical-too. Accessed 1 June 2025.

8   Stern, Joseph D. "The Benefits of Crying." *Joseph D. Stern, MD*, 9 Jan. 2023, www.josephsternmd.com/2023/01/09/the-benefits-of-crying/. Accessed 1 June 2025.

9   Sillis, Lauren, et al. "Association between Grief and Somatic Complaints in Bereaved University and College Students." *MDPI*, 24 Sept. 2022, www.mdpi.com/1660-4601/19/19/12108. Accessed 22 June 2025.

10 Brewer, Mark. "Ecotherapy and Supporting Your Grief." *Ecorial*, 24 Sept. 2022, ecorial.org/blogs/articles/ecotherapy-supporting-your-grief-through-nature. Accessed 22 June 2025.

11 DePew, Dave. "Moving Through Grief: Using Exercise and Positive Reflection to Heal." *Grinder Gym*, 3 Oct. 2024, grindergym.com/moving-through-grief-using-exercise-and-positive-reflection-to-heal/. Accessed 22 June 2025.

12 "The Healing Power of Music." *Weill Cornell Medicine – Qatar*, 15 June 2025, qatar-weill.cornell.edu/media-center/news/story/the-healing-power-of-music. Accessed 22 June 2025.

13 Victor, David. "How Music Helps People Heal: The Therapeutic Power of Music." *Harmony & Healing*, 19 June 2024, www.harmonyandhealing.org/how-music-helps-people-heal/. Accessed 22 June 2025.

14 Blakemore, Erin. "Concerts Strike a Chord with Mental Health." *Colorado News and Culture from MSU Denver*, 1 Aug. 2023, red.msudenver.edu/2023/summer-concerts-strike-a-chord-with-mental-health/. Accessed 22 June 2025.

15 Brodie, Jessica. "What Is the Garden of Gethsemane and Why Was It So Crucial to Jesus' Life?" *Bible Study Tools*, 27 Mar. 2024, www.biblestudytools.com/bible-study/topical-studies/what-is-the-garden-of-gethsemane-and-why-was-it-so-crucial-to-jesus-life.html. Accessed 20 June 2025.

16 *ESV Study Bible*, 479.

17 *ESV Study Bible*, 110.

18 "Why Kintsugi." *The Kintsugi Village*, 10 Mar. 2025, kintsugivillage.org/why-kintsugi/.